*R*alph writes, "The writing in the classroom can only be as good as the literature that buoys it up." And I might say, "The *teaching* of writing in the classroom can only be as good as the *professional* literature that buoys it up." For me as a teacher of writing, *What a Writer Needs* has been a buoy—and an anchor holding that buoy fast—for almost twenty years. I cannot imagine the teacher I would be if I had not read this book. More than any other professional book, *What a Writer Needs* taught me things about writing—concrete, specific things—that empowered me and made a real difference in my day-to-day teaching. I was floundering about without an anchor until I read this book.

In this new edition, Ralph writes, "We need to think hard about how we talk about writing—to our colleagues, to our students, to ourselves." This is what this classic book gave me as a teacher of writing when I read the first edition almost twenty years ago. *What a Writer Needs* helped me talk about writing in new ways because it helped me *think* about writing in new ways. This one book probably did more to build my knowledge base about writing than any other. I was empowered by what I learned from Ralph, and I still pull from that knowledge base today in countless writing conferences and whole-class lessons. If I had a quarter for every time I've helped a young writer understand, *the bigger the issue, the smaller you write,* I'd be wealthy! I truly feel my work is grounded in the fundamental ideas I learned from *What a Writer Needs*, and reading the second edition, I realize it's as relevant today as it was then.

—**Katie Wood Ray**
author of *About the Authors*

In this new edition, I was reminded that I need to make time to read all sorts of books about whatever interests me, that whatever we learn for our own real purposes will find its way into our writing as well as our teaching. Mostly, however, Ralph helped me understand in whole new ways what we need—what *I* need—in order to write and to teach our students to write. We need to love language and give room to play with it on the page. We need mentors who can show us the moves and give us the courage and wisdom to continue writing (and teaching) when we begin to lose faith in the talent we are still nurturing. We need permission to take risks—and to let *students* take the risks that will reward them with a sense of ownership that comes from doing the work of writers, from working *as* writers. And we need time: to listen, to learn, to read and reflect, to write and rewrite, and rewrite again once we finally know what we are trying to say.

What we really need, however, is Ralph Fletcher. Since we cannot bring him home with us to help us write our own stories or help us teach our students to write theirs, we are fortunate enough to have the next best thing—this book. For that, *and* for Ralph Fletcher, for his books, his stories about his family, the joy that shines through on every page of this book—I am very grateful and a better teacher to boot.

—**Jim Burke**
author of *The English Teacher's Companion*

I have read—and bought—most of the books on writing published since I was in high school half a century ago and most of the books on teaching writing since 1963, and I have not read another book that does what this one does.

Fletcher serves many readers, a professional challenge in itself. *What a Writer Needs* will be a valuable text and resource book for the teacher who wants to write; it will be just as valuable for the teacher who does not want to write but wants to teach writing; it will also be valuable for students in kindergarten through twelfth grade as its lessons are passed down through teachers and in many cases learned directly from Fletcher as teachers read from the book or pass it to individual students.

—**Donald M. Murray**
excerpt from first edition foreword of *What a Writer Needs*

RALPH FLETCHER

WHAT A WRITER NEEDS

SECOND EDITION

*With new chapters on **nonfiction** and **revision***

HEINEMANN
Portsmouth, NH

Heinemann
361 Hanover Street
Portsmouth, NH 03801–3912
www.heinemann.com

Offices and agents throughout the world

The author and publisher wish to thank those who have generously given permission to reprint borrowed material in this book:

Poem "Mother Nature" by Gary Snyder. Reprinted by permission of New Directions Publishing Corporation.

Excerpt from *The Two of Them* by Aliki. Copyright © 1979 by Aliki Brandenberg. Reprinted by permission of HarperCollins Publishers.

credits continue on p. vi

Library of Congress Cataloging-in-Publication Data
Fletcher, Ralph J.
  What a writer needs / Ralph Fletcher. — Second edition.
       pages cm
  Includes bibliographical references and index.
  ISBN-13: 978-0-325-04666-2
  1. English language—Composition and exercises—Study and teach-
ing (Elementary)—United States. 2. English language—Composition and
exercises—Study and teaching (Secondary)—United States. I. Title.
  LB1576.F483 2013
  372.6—dc23   2012045231

Acquisitions Editor: Holly Kim Price
Production Editor: Patricia Adams
Cover and Interior Designs: Monica Ann Crigler
Typesetter: Valerie Levy/Drawing Board Studios
Manufacturing: Steve Bernier

Printed in the United States of America on acid-free paper
21 20 19 18 17 VP 3 4 5 6 7

For my father
Ralph Joseph Fletcher

CONTENTS

ACKNOWLEDGMENTS . . . . *IX*

INTRODUCTION *1*

PART ONE *Essentials*

1. MENTORS *9*
2. FREEZING TO THE FACE *21*
3. A LOVE OF WORDS *31*

PART TWO *The Craft*

4. THE ART OF SPECIFICITY *45*
5. CREATING A CHARACTER *55*
6. VOICE *67*
7. BEGINNINGS *81*
8. ENDINGS *93*
9. TENSION *104*
10. A SENSE OF PLACE *118*
11. A PLAYFULNESS WITH TIME *127*
12. UNFORGETTABLE LANGUAGE *144*
13. WRITING NONFICTION *153*
14. REVISION *165*

UN-FINAL THOUGHTS *177*

APPENDIX *183*

INDEX *208*

Acknowledgments

AFTER THE BEATLES BROKE UP, Paul McCartney was asked if the band would ever get back together. He replied: "I don't think so. You can't reheat a soufflé."

This is one of my all-time favorite quotes, and I think it's pertinent to anyone trying to write a new edition of a book, even a mortal non-Beatle like me. How do I update what I still consider my best book on teaching writing? I am grateful to have had Holly Price, my Heinemann editor, to help me with this challenge. Holly was the co-pilot who helped me navigate the tricky shoals of this project. She provided just the right touch; I found her judgments invaluable at crucial points.

My friend Kate Montgomery was a great early sounding board when we began to envision this new edition. The whole Heinemann team was terrific. And I'll forever be grateful to Dawn Boyer, who was my editor for the first edition of this book.

Thanks always to Philippa.

Thanks to my friend Carol Wilcox, who did yeoman's (yeowoman's?) work updating the Appendix for this second edition.

This book was fed by many deep professional roots.

Over the years my ideas about writing have been refined through intense, ongoing conversations with many people including Carl Anderson, Kathy Collins, Chris Crutcher, Smokey Daniels, Dan Feigelson, Jane Hansen, Stef Harvey, Sharon Hill, Martha Horn, Peter Johnston, Ellin Keene, Mike McCormick, Tom Newkirk, Katie Wood Ray, Tom Romano, Jon Scieszka, Lad Tobin, Jim Vopat, Janet Wong, and Steve Zemelman. My wife, JoAnn Portalupi, and I have had innumerable conversations and collaborations concerning this and other books on this subject.

My ideas on writing have also been enriched by many fine books on the teaching of writing by the likes of Carl Anderson, Jeff Anderson, Nancie Atwell, Aimee Buckner, Carolyn Coman, Ruth Culham, Brock Dethier, Kelly Gallagher, Mary Ellen Giacobbe, Georgia Heard, Martha Horn, Lester Laminack, Linda Rief, Regie Routman, and Franki Sibberson. I'd be remiss not to mention William Zinsser, Stephen King, and Anne Lamott, who raised the bar and showed me what a book on writing might look like.

Thanks to my teacher friends—Patrick Allen, Gresham Brown, Jody Chang, Paul Crivelli, Kathleen Fay, Jan Furuta, Shelley Harwayne, Anna Lee Lum, Miki Maeshiro, Katy Mayo-Hudson, Kate Morris, Carrie Tenebrini, Sara Tillett, Suzanne Whaley, and JoAnn Wong-Kam—for helping me to keep it real.

Thanks to Lucy Calkins. You were there in the beginning when I was at the Teachers College Writing Project. You believed in me 100 percent, which is not something I can say about many people. Shelley Harwayne was another important mentor of mine at the Writing Project.

I have been inspired by the late Don Graves, who fearlessly led the charge for more authentic writing instruction in schools.

I write in the shadow of the late Don Murray. Reading Don's books on writing forever altered my view of writing and teaching writing. I first became aware of Don as a famous writer who won the Pulitzer Prize, but later I was lucky enough to get to know him personally. I was honored when Don wrote the foreword to the first edition of *What a Writer Needs*; I like to think he sprinkled a little Murray dust on it. I sorely miss Don, but he's not really gone—his ideas on writing continue to inspire my work.

As for a few deeper roots, personal roots . . .

Ever since I can remember, my parents were ravenous readers (as are all the people in my family). My father still polishes off a couple novels each week. He and my late mother have always been unapologetic fans of mine. They gave me unwavering love and support.

What a privilege it has been to watch my sons Taylor, Adam, Robert, and Joseph walk out of their childhoods and begin to make their way in the world.

Finally, I am thankful to my wife JoAnn, for being the strong center of our family, for being such a terrific mother to our boys, for helping me survive life's difficult challenges, for spending peaceful hours with me picking stones at Herring Cove Beach on Campobello Island . . . and too many other ways to mention.

$\mathcal{I}$NTRODUCTION

IT HAPPENED in a classroom one frigid November morning, not far from Albany, New York, when the clouds were hanging low and steely in the sky. At precisely 11:03 the third-grade teacher glimpsed something, a fraying hint of whiteness outside the classroom window.

"It's starting to snow!" she said to her class. The kids blinked and looked up. "Come here. Over to the window. We'll open the blinds up and take a good look at it."

The children hurried over, eager to eyeball the year's first snowfall. Innumerable fat flakes parachuting down. One boy held back and stayed at his desk.

"Come on, Brent," the teacher urged. "Join us."

But Brent was adamant. "Don't do it!" he cried to the other kids. "Don't look! She'll make us write!"

This is one of my favorite stories—it reminds me not to get too evangelical about teaching writing. Teaching writing is hard work. As writing teachers, we come upon every imaginable kind of thorny problem: students who hate to write, who lack confidence and write poorly, who love to write but can't read back what they have written, who can't spell, can't conjugate, can't punctuate . . .

Most children do learn to write, more or less. But how do we, as teachers and/or parents, sustain and extend this natural development? Much of their growth will come through independent work: writing a great deal, reading widely and deeply, discovering useful writing strategies borrowed from professional writers.

But there is no way around it: Our students will also learn to write from us.

Writing teachers draw upon three distinct areas of expertise. We must know our students. We must know how to teach. But it's important that we know something about writing itself. Many fine texts on teaching writing have explored the nuts and bolts of the writing workshop. This book concerns itself with the art and craft of writing itself. I hope readers of this book will get a better grasp of how writing works, both in its parts and as a whole.

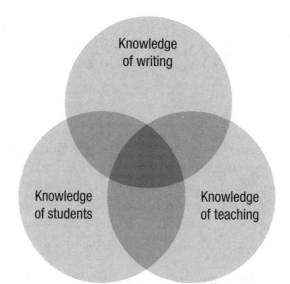

Odysseus learned to steer his ship between Scylla and Charybdis, mythological monsters who bedeviled and devoured all sailors who dared attempt that narrow passage. In this book I imagine myself trying a similarly tricky navigation. On one side, the book risks running aground on the rocks of dense theory. Writing is a complicated business that can get you neck-deep into a scholarly rumination on linguistics, etymology, or semiotics if you're not careful. A writer might even select a single element of writing, such as *voice* or *character,* and expand it into an entire book.

On the other side, I knew for certain I did not want to write a writing recipe book: one fresh lead, a dash of suspense, a pinch of voice, etc. Writing just doesn't work that way.

I have tried to find the middle ground: a practical book about writing. I have included strategies that a writer might use immediately in his or her own writing. Not all writers make good writing teachers (and vice versa). While apprenticing as a writer, and gathering an impressive portfolio of rejection slips, I cherished the advice from writers I respected who were willing to share their secrets with me, who could help me find a way through the dizzying complexities of this craft to what Donald Murray calls the "unifying simplicities" that lie underneath.

This is no recipe book; I have tried not to be formulaic. Rather, I want to suggest the richness of options, the myriad possibilities open to the writer at any given moment. Young writers need to know what can be done with language. The strategies and suggestions included here might be thought of as the colors on an artist's palette. The artist begins by learning color—

primary and secondary, highlight and shade—but this is only the beginning. Ultimately, it's up to the artist to decide when (and if) to use a particular color in a painting.

Any writing text must include concrete examples. I have drawn them from several sources—my own writing, the writing of students and teachers, and literature: fiction, poetry, articles, and picture books. These examples were not selected for grade-level applicability; some are probably not appropriate for children at all. Don Graves was right: As writing/reading teachers, we must begin with our own literacy. Even with very young children, we need to bring a wealth of knowledge to our understanding of their writing. The examples in this book were selected to broaden and deepen that knowledge.

Many teachers have come to recognize that picture books can be terrific tools for exploring writing, not just for young children but with writers of all ages. A picture book like *Owl Moon* by Jane Yolen is subtle, beautifully written, and eminently rereadable. The best books of this genre have a lovely transparency that makes them perfect for talking about writing. They contain all the classical literary elements (leads, conflict, protagonist, resolution, etc.) without the numbing volume of details, incidents, and characters that make it nearly impossible for students to grasp such elements by themselves.

Writing this book, and answering for myself the questions it raised, helped distill my own ideas about writing. What are the fundamental elements of good writing? Is it possible to prioritize (hate that word) them? Is voice more important than character? Should I include specific writing exercises for the young writer to practice?

The question of writing exercises reminds me of my first overnight camping trip that I took with the Boy Scouts. After all the tents had been set up, the oldest boys in our troop gathered the youngest boys together. Eight of us, Tenderfeet all, gazed up expectantly at the bigger boys.

"We've got a problem—we're missing some important stuff," one of the oldest boys said in a low and serious voice. "We're going to have a tough time without it, too."

"Yeah," another boy said. "We forgot to bring the bacon-stretcher. Can't cook bacon over a campfire without it."

"That's not all," another boy said glumly. "There's the sky hook. Kenny, I can't believe you left that at home."

"Bad news," the first boy said. "We're going to need that stuff. Look, I'm going to split you kids up. You four go over to that camp and ask the Scout Master if we can borrow their bacon-stretcher. You four go the other way, to that campsite just over that ridge. See if they'll let us use their sky hook. At least 'til tomorrow. See if they have an extra one."

I felt proud to be trusted to take part in such an important mission. I went with the kids in search of the bacon-stretcher. The Scout Master of the troop camped directly next to us listened carefully to our request, rubbed his forehead, shook his head solemnly, and sent us to another camp. From there we were sent to another camp. It took nearly two hours of trudging around before someone mercifully let us in on the joke.

True, not all writing exercises are as maliciously useless as sky hooks and bacon-stretchers. But many are. I watched a teacher read *The Lorax* by Dr. Seuss to her students. These were big kids, eighth graders, and they were riveted. She had them.

"Now, I want you to write a letter to Mr. Once-ler," she told the students. "Tell him how you feel about the way he's been chopping down all the trees."

That broke the spell. The kids sighed, slumped. They knew only too well Mr. Once-ler was a fictitious character. No one would read the letters. The exercise lacked any authentic purpose.

I know several writers who found certain writing exercises helpful in college or graduate writing programs, and I do include a few in this book. But I think we need to be wary of them, particularly for elementary or middle school writers. Here's my belief: You don't learn to write by going through a series of preset writing exercises. You learn to write by grappling with a real subject that truly matters to you.

In the first part of this book I explore the essential conditions that allowed me to become a writer—finding mentors I could look up to, learning to take risks, building on a love of words—and how these conditions might nourish young writers in a classroom setting. In Part Two, I take a closer look at a dozen tools that writers use nearly every day: balancing the specific with the general, creating character and a sense of place, beginnings and endings, juggling the issue of time, and so forth.

I tried to choose those elements of writing that are not specific to any one genre but could help writers develop their craft in many different kinds of writing. Developing character may be a prime concern of the fiction writer or journalist, but it can also be crucially important to the historian or poet. Journalists do not have a monopoly on the use of research, nor do poets with metaphor.

One danger of having discrete chapters in a book such as this one is that it may suggest a segmented, compartmentalized approach to writing. In fact, no element of writing can exist in isolation. If a poem or an essay works at all, it works as an organic unit, with every part contributing almost invisibly to the total effect of the piece. Every part, every *word,* depends upon its relationship to the whole. When we talk about the different elements or components of writing, it may be helpful to conceive of them as different lenses—fresh perspectives, through which we can view the gestalt and understand more clearly how writing works.

I once heard Gary Snyder read the following poem:

Mother Nature

She is not a sheath:
She is a quiver.

Snyder has had a profound effect on my own poetry, so it was with some trepidation that I approached him after the reading and introduced myself. For me, at least, it was a heart-stopping literary moment: The man standing right next to Snyder was none other than Allen Ginsberg. Ginsberg's eyes twinkled while he listened.

"I didn't understand that poem 'Mother Nature,'" I confessed.

"Well, do you know the Latin word for sheath?" Snyder asked me impatiently.

"No, I don't know Latin," I admitted. Snyder looked piteously, first at Ginsberg, then back to me.

"Look, you've got to know Latin if you want to write poetry. Look it up." He sighed. "A sheath holds but one thing, right? A quiver holds many arrows. Mother Nature holds many things . . ."

I retreated, enlightened if chagrined, but those words come back to me now. In writing this book, I created a file with sections for the various elements of writing: BEGINNINGS, ENDINGS, CHARACTER, TIME, SETTING, DETAILS, etc. If I found a piece of writing with a wonderful ending, I'd make a copy and file it in the appropriate section. But many bits of writing did not fit smoothly into one particular category. These pieces of writing, like Mother Nature in Snyder's poem, contained many things and resisted my attempt to boil them down to one essential element. Consider this passage from William Steig's *Amos and Boris,* a terrific picture book about the friendship between a whale (Boris) and a mouse (Amos):

> Swimming along, sometimes at great speed, sometimes slowly and leisurely, sometimes resting and exchanging ideas, sometimes stopping to sleep, it took them a week to reach Amos's home shore. During that time they developed

a deep admiration for one another. Boris admired the delicacy, the quivering daintiness, the light touch, the small voice, the gemlike radiance of the mouse. Amos admired the bulk, the grandeur, the power, the purpose, the rich voice, and the abounding friendliness of the whale.

A wonderful passage, but where should I file it? Characterization? Tension? Sparkling language? Words? Humor? Voice? Compare and contrast? This passage is a quiver—no matter how hard I try, it refuses to be a sheath.

It is inevitable that teachers use labels or pet names when talking about writing. My colleague Karen Howell asks children to reread and look for the *hot spot* in their stories. This phrase gives the novice writer a new way to reread a narrative. I have suggested that students might conceive of a story as a river going over a waterfall.

"Be careful you don't start your story too far upstream," I cautioned one group of fifth graders. "When I write, I usually want the reader to be able to hear the faint roar from that waterfall right at the beginning."

Metaphors like these can help students internalize complex writing issues by rooting the issue in a concrete, sensuous image.

However, labels can also be dangerous. They risk cheapening the prose or poem by diminishing our thinking about it rather than opening it up. A story, after all, is not a river coursing over a waterfall. In most ways, narratives and rivers obey laws quite distinct from one another. Writing teachers need to be careful when using verbal shorthand to talk about complicated subjects. We need to think hard about how we talk about writing—to our colleagues, to our students, to ourselves. Language, as the linguists tell us, is also the language of thought. In the end, the words we use to explain such concepts to our students will be the words they use to explain the concepts to themselves.

PART **ONE**

Essentials

One

MENTORS

I have come to the frightening conclusion that I am the decisive element in the classroom. It's my personal approach that creates the climate. It's my daily mood that makes the weather. As a teacher, I possess tremendous power to make a child's life miserable or joyous. I can be a tool of torture or an instrument of inspiration. I can humiliate or humor, hurt or heal.

— HAIM GINOTT

IN COLLEGE I took a creative writing seminar with the novelist Calder Willingham. The man was a real pro: he had already published ten novels as well as screenplays for *Little Big Man* and *The Graduate.*

Calder Willingham. The very name sounded literary. He was a Southerner, a tall, red-haired man with gangly limbs and a bourbon nose. We met at an off-campus apartment the college rented for him every Wednesday night. There were ten students in the class. He always had on hand plenty of rolls, cold cuts, chips, pickles, beer, wine, and Teacher's Scotch. Class went from 7 to 9 P.M. But we rarely left before 11, and many of us left a bit unsteadily at that.

Willingham dissected our stories, three per night. We loved this man; we soaked up every facial expression he made in response to our work, his most casual aside. He had emphatic tastes about literature—prejudices, he would be the first to admit—and did not shy away from sharing them with us. It didn't take much to touch off some of Willingham's diatribes.

"Tell me a *story,*" he'd thunder. "I don't care how smart you are, how philosophical you get. If you don't tell me a story I'm not going to want to read more than a few pages. And beware 'purple prose'—the disease of modern writing, if you ask me. When you write you should be asking your-self: *What* am I trying to say? And say it."

On the night of our last class, Willingham sat before us in a tweed jacket and black tie. He held a stack of long white envelopes in his hand.

"I didn't teach this class for the money," he said softly. "I decided to teach this class to repay a favor. When I was a young writer, James T. Farrell took me under his wing a little bit and helped me out. He told me, 'Someday, you might be able to help out a struggling writer yourself.' That's why I'm teach-ing this class. What he said is still true today, maybe truer than ever. There are a lot of young writers out there. Someday you might be able to lend them a hand."

He took out the envelopes and lay them in his lap.

"Here's what I've done. The college has paid me sixteen hundred bucks to teach this course. I've taken that amount and subtracted everything I spent on booze and whatnot. That leaves about a thousand dollars, even. What I've done is divide that amount among the members of this class. Nobody is get-ting less than a B. A B gets you fifty bucks. An A gets you a hundred bucks, and an A with a citation will get you a hundred and fifty bucks."

We gasped, laughed.

"First, Mr. Shnayerson . . ." Willingham said, clearing his throat and smil-ing to himself as he fingered the first envelope.

I'll never forget Calder Willingham (though I'm not sure I endorse monetary rewards for writers in our classrooms). His words are well worth remembering for all of us who work with young writers: "There's a lot of young writers out there. Someday you might be able to lend them a hand."

Our classrooms are filled with students desperate for adults who care about writing and books as much as they do. As teachers, we find ourselves in a unique position to be mentors for these emerging writers. If for whatever reason we cannot do so, we should encourage our students to find someone else—an uncle, a librarian, another teacher—who can fill that crucial role.

When I first envisioned this book, I imagined tucking a chapter on men-tors near the back, just before the Appendix, perhaps. It seemed like a fine, if predictable way to finish—young writers need adults who can help them reach new horizons, and so forth. It didn't take long for me to revise my thinking. It struck me how often I go back to the advice of those adults who shaped me as a young writer. No, the mentor chapter would not suffice as an after-dinner mint: It had to be an integral part of the main course. For one thing, such a chapter would allow me to grapple with the ghosts of all those people who most powerfully sculpted my psyche—for better and for worse—as a young writer.

Mrs. Damon was my first-grade teacher. The photograph of our class, where I am firmly wedged between Steve Fishman and Pamela Coyne, reveals Mrs. Damon to be a gray-haired woman, slightly stocky, in a starchy white blouse. All business, this woman. Mrs. Damon was more than the first writing mentor I encountered at school. For me, Mrs. Damon *was* school. Her moods, her high standards, created the emotional landscape through which I moved and thought and labored that first school year.

I revered this woman. It pained me to live with the knowledge that while I excelled in many areas, I consistently let Mrs. Damon down in one: My handwriting was horrific. I simply could not get my fingers to make the pencil dance the way a pencil should dance. My letters leaned, wandered, wobbled, and trembled so violently even I could not read them most of the time. I drooled over the perfectly printed papers the girls in our class produced with such apparent effortlessness. No matter how hard I tried, I could not replicate anything even approaching their work. In that classroom, writing *was* penmanship, and no paper of mine ever received higher than a C.

One day I got a paper back with a D– scrawled on the top. (The minus next to the D seemed to slope down, a grieving elephant with a drooped trunk.) I took the paper home, crumpled it up, and hid it under a rock that was painted white in the front corner of our yard. Later, I retrieved the wrinkled paper and shamefully showed it to my parents.

Mrs. Damon took a vigilant stance toward my penmanship problem. She made it *our* problem, and set me to work on rectifying it. My nightly homework assignments included practicing the alphabet by printing all twenty-six letters five times on five separate sheets of paper. Each sheet had to be signed by my mother and handed in promptly the following morning.

One afternoon Mrs. Damon took me aside and looked deeply into my eyes.

"Listen, Ralph," she said softly. "You're going to have to work harder on this. You've got sloppy penmanship, and sloppy penmanship means a sloppy personality."

A sloppy personality! Had the words come from anyone else, I might have been able to shrug them off. From her, I could not. Mrs. Damon, how could you say such a thing to me? It was you who taught me to add and subtract, to recite the Pledge of Allegiance, to sing "America the Beautiful." You taught me to read. I trusted you: I listened. I could as easily ignore your words as my own mother's. Your judgment bore deep holes in my soul. Years later I would learn the ins and outs of motor coordination, large and small.

I would learn that in kindergarten and first grade the fine-motor coordination of boys is roughly one year behind the fine-motor coordination of girls. I would learn that a writer might indeed have ambitions beyond neat penmanship. But in first grade I was branded with a sloppy personality. And I never quite got over it.

During the years that followed, I endured what passed for writing in school. All the important writing I did took place at home. I started writing little books, a series about a baseball rookie named Carlos who breaks into the majors to tremendous acclaim. Carlos was a phenom: the kid could do no wrong. Veteran pitchers scratched their heads, concocted new pitches like "space balls" and "submarine balls," anything to get Carlos out. This was a natural topic for me because sports books were just about all I was reading: *The Willie Mays Story, My Turn at Bat* by Ted Williams, *It's Good to Be Alive* by Roy Campanella.

By high school I had become a serious reader: Novels were my mentors. Anything by Poe, Hemingway, Fitzgerald, Dostoyevsky, Dickens. *One Flew Over the Cuckoo's Nest* by Ken Kesey. *Going After Cacciato* by Tim O'Brien. Tolkien and Frank Norris. Brautigan and D. H. Lawrence. I'd gulp them down with indiscriminate naïveté—pop books and classics—before passing them on to my younger brothers and sisters. I watched my brother Jim become so enchanted by Gabriel García Márquez's masterpiece, *One Hundred Years of Solitude,* that in an act of near masochistic discipline he rationed himself to twenty-five pages per night to make the book last as long as possible. When the book finally came my way I discovered that I lacked his mettle; I consumed the thick novel in four or five lengthy swallows.

Books like these tore me up inside. What an incredible thing, to be able to affect adults and children, total strangers, people in other countries, with nothing but words, words forged out of your own experience, your own heart, your own imagination!

In graduate school I took several courses with Richard Price. He was just a few years older than me (mentors don't necessarily have to be old, white-haired, bearded) and had just finished his fourth novel, *The Breaks.* He would later go on to Hollywood to write *The Color of Money, Clockers, Ransom,* and many other screenplays. He also wrote for the HBO series, *The Wire.* Price's seminars were dominated by his wit, which could be scathing at times, though he generally delivered his most barbed lines with smiling good humor.

"Your narrator needs an alarm clock," he told one student. "He's sleep-walking through your story. Wake him up!"

"You're telling us on page nine that the mother still misses her kid," Price barked another time. "Hey, guess what? We got that on page *two.* Come on. Trust your reader. Where are you going with this?"

Certain writers in the seminar (myself included) tended to get overly didactic in our stories, or sink our sentences with too much heavy-handed philosophizing. One day Price took issue with it.

"You're getting awfully preachy in this story," he told one of my peers. "A lot of writers here have the same problem. If you want to send a message, go to Western Union."

Everyone laughed. The remark hit home.

A mentor relationship between an experienced writer and novice can take many forms. But my own mentors, and the teachers I know who are real mentors to the young writers they work with, have certain things in common.

A MENTOR HAS HIGH STANDARDS

I once spent a week in New Orleans with the late poet Robert Stock, a contemporary of Jack Kerouac and Kenneth Rexroth. Stock was a tall man with long silver hair and a beautiful, ruined face. I would stay up late with him while he managed to drink gin, watch old movies, and read poetry in the original Brazilian, all at the same time. He was very generous to me and encouraged me to show him some poetry I had written.

"I like this poem," I said, "but it's not quite done. There's one word here, in this line, that isn't quite right."

He burst out laughing.

"I must have thrown away a hundred poems for that reason," he said. "Because a single word wasn't right."

Stock's fanatical perfectionism made an indelible impression on me. A mentor does not praise mediocre work. A mentor knows the sound and the feel of language skillfully used. The novice writer, who is becoming alive to the possibilities of language, respects that.

A mentor's high standards inspire a young writer not to lower his or her own standards. When I was just beginning my career as a writer I wrote to a friend, the poet David Fisher. I shared the good news that I had just had an article accepted for publication in *Cosmopolitan* magazine. But Fisher was not impressed.

"Forget *Cosmopolitan,*" he wrote back to me. "Think Thomas Mann. Think Virginia Woolf."

A MENTOR BUILDS ON STRENGTHS

"Kill your darlings," Richard Price used to say, urging us to discover our own bad writing tendencies and ruthlessly ferret them out. This suggestion was helpful to semi-proficient writers in a graduate seminar. But exhorting very young writers (or students who write without confidence) to kill their darlings may do more harm than good: Once the "darlings" have been killed off in a student's writing there may not be much left that is still alive.

Like a good music teacher, a writing teacher endures the bad melodies and shaky rhythms, stays patient, and picks out moments when the writing works well. It might be but a sentence—"The rollercoaster went upside down and stopped like a bat hanging from a tree"—or a single phrase. Even in a "bad" piece of writing the mentor reaches into the chaos, finds a place where the writing works, pulls it from the wreckage, names it, and makes the writer aware of this emerging skill with words. Careful praise of this kind can fuel a writer for a long time.

Most students write far better than they will ever know. We have to let children in on the secret of how powerfully they write. We need to let them take inspiration from what they already do well. Consider this disturbing poem by a third-grade boy from Queens, something that might never get published in a conventional press or magazine because of its searing honesty.

My Life

My life is like
a garbage truck:
Saturdays and Sundays off.
Monday
Tuesday
Wednesday
Thursday
Friday
they haul you
away.

The following poem by a second grader in New York City was inspired by Nan Fry's poem, "The Apple":

The Corn

The

    corn

        is

           like

        a

           maze

through all its kernels on the cob.
In the middle of the holes
there is darkness
and over it
the sunny bright sky.

What a clever pun on the word *maze!* Deliberate? Of course not. But skilled writers learn how to take advantage of the pleasant surprises that crop up in their writing. The teacher pointed it out to her; they looked up the word "maize" in the dictionary. Before long the girl was beaming as if she had planned the pun herself.

I read *The Two of Them* by Aliki to a class of Long Island second graders. The children and I discussed the book and, later, Christine Martinez wrote this tribute to her grandfather:

> My grandpa gave Heather my sister a necklace and when I was born my grandpa gave me a ring and last year it fit me and this year he died. He died at the beginning of the year. When I went to his house we played cards and we also played a guessing game. And we planted flowers. And when he died my grandma told me that the flowers died. I was the one who cryed the most. My mom's friend Ilean took us for some pizza, and to see home alone and then to friendlys. He didn't want a funeral so that night we went to see him before he went away. I bought some flowers for him and I used all of my money and I'm still broke. And when I was born he said thank god it's another girl the army can't take her away.

I am haunted by the sentence near the end—"I bought some flowers for him and I used all of my money and I'm still broke"—which suggests layers of meaning the young writer is unaware of, particularly with the use of the word "broke." A mentor can highlight such fortunate accidents for the young writer.

A mentor builds on strengths, often seeing more in a student's work than the student sees. My friend Robert Cohen, author of *Inspired Sleep,* once said to me: "The lines in your poem have lots of energy. Texture. The lines are dense. But in your prose writing the sentences tend to be flatter, smoother, more transparent. If I were you I'd try to put more of the dense, textured language that's in your poetry into your prose."

This advice literally changed me as a writer. But it could only have been given by someone who knew my work well. And it was easy to take because he prefaced his suggestion by first commenting on what he perceived as a strength in my writing.

A MENTOR VALUES ORIGINALITY AND DIVERSITY

I watched Artie Voigt work with fifteen young writers during a two-week writing institute for children and teachers in Manhassett, New York.

"Is your class coming together?" one teacher asked him.

"I don't *want* them to come together," Artie cheerfully replied. "I want the kids to keep going in whatever direction they need to go."

A writing teacher will challenge students to attain a species of excellence according to particular beliefs about writing. This cannot be otherwise; it's hard to teach what you don't believe. The teacher, however, may encounter a student whose writing differs dramatically from the teacher's idea of excellent writing. A true mentor will try not to penalize the student or clone a duplicate of himself. Rather, a mentor is forever alive to the possibility of something new and distinctly original.

Anne, a teacher I work with, wrote a series of stories when she was in fifth grade. The teacher read them and, realizing that she didn't quite know what to do with them, passed them on to a local author. The author telephoned Anne.

"Did this all really happen?" the author asked.

"No," Anne admitted. "I made most of it up."

"Well, you're the best damn liar I've ever come across," the author retorted. "Keep writing!"

A mentor possesses an inner honesty, an ability to recognize that the novice's different style of writing may camouflage a deeper truth: The novice writes better than the teacher. It requires courage and real humility to recognize this and to step graciously out of the way.

"That's the most humbling thing about teaching," one teacher confided to me. "You teach some kids who are just plain smarter—some of them a *lot* smarter—than you are."

A MENTOR ENCOURAGES STUDENTS TO TAKE RISKS

A kindergarten teacher is preparing her children for a visit to a dinosaur exhibit.

"What do you think 'extinct' means?" she asks.

"I think it means the dinosaurs *smelled*," one boy says. "You know, like *stink*."

"No," the teacher replies with a grin, "but that's smart thinking. Great guess, Ron!"

"Wait, I think I know," the same boy says. "It's *ex*-tinct, so it must mean that the dinosaurs *don't* smell. Right?"

"Ron, that is so smart!" the teacher says to him.

This teacher places a higher value on Ron's habits of thought, his willingness to apply his knowledge to brand new information, than she does on his getting the correct answer.

Risk, as educator Patrick Shannon points out, is crucially important: Risk allows children to outgrow themselves. But schools today don't go nearly far enough to encourage students to take risks in their learning. Compare Ron to the fourth-grade girl who runs up to her teacher waving a paper back and forth, asking: "Is this poem right or is it wrong?"

Any writer who labors under such a right/wrong schema will never allow herself the fluency and playfulness, the time and perseverance she will need over the long haul to become a skillful writer.

Novice writers often go through a great deal of turmoil, an era of rich experimentation, before attaining any degree of confidence as a writer. This may include physically copying a short story out of a book, attempting a free-verse poem instead of a rhyming couplet, playing with various leads, aping the style of a favorite writer, free-writing, using longer sentences, trying out more complex vocabulary.

It's important to recognize the critical place this kind of experimentation has in the writer's development. A mentor will not penalize the student whose risks do not immediately produce a superbly written essay or report. We need to redefine the success ethic, not just in writing classes but during the entire school day, to mean not only "Did you get it right?" but also "Did you take a chance? Did you try something you've never tried before?"

A MENTOR IS PASSIONATE

Passion remains the most important quality the mentor has to offer. When we think back on those teachers we looked up to, we don't always remember exactly what they taught. Above everything, we remember passion. Fire. At Dartmouth, I took Peter Bien's terrific course that compared James Joyce and Nikos Kazantzakis. On the last day of the class Bien, a balding, bespectacled man and leading authority on Kazantzakis, put down his notes and spoke to us directly, ending with a plea that we all "keep reading, keep buying books." He stopped. We looked at the clock: time was up. The course was over. All seventy students stood up spontaneously and gave him a rousing ovation. What were we cheering about, anyway? Not his sense of humor, which was fine, if a bit dry. Not his scholarship, which was impeccable. We were relishing this man's passion for ideas.

After watching his daughter Susannah learn how to sail, Artie Voigt commented to me: "It's such a great feeling to watch someone else enjoying what you love to do yourself." Through the relationship with a novice, a mentor gets to experience the thrill of the craft (as well as its pain) all over again. In this way the mentor's passion never gets spent: it gets renewed again and again through the mentoring relationship.

MENTORS CAN BE BOOKS AS WELL AS PEOPLE

Not all readers are writers, but all writers are readers. This becomes apparent in the classroom—the best writers are almost always the kids who have been read to, who love books, who have "book language" alive inside them. When teachers share potent texts with their students, and provide time to really talk about them, the quality of student writing can only improve. The writing in the classroom can only be as good as the literature that buoys it up.

All writers are guided and inspired by the books they read. This is a mysterious process, and I believe it's less about writerly craft or technique than about raw emotional force.

"You can't write until you have been flattened by a book," Stephen King writes in *On Writing*. I have been flattened by innumerable books including *Hunger* by Knut Hamsun, *Angle of Repose* by Wallace Stegner, *Bel Canto* by Ann Patchett, *The Time-Traveler's Wife* by Audrey Niffenegger, *Sometimes a Great Notion* by Ken Kesey, and many more. Novels like these, as well as countless poems and essays, have inspired me in ways both big and small, and provided a crucial lift for my own writing.

But it's important to remember that this lift doesn't happen instantaneously. Don Murray used to teach a two-semester course on writing at the University of New Hampshire. He noticed that often he would introduce a strategy in the first semester, but his students wouldn't start using it in their own writing until the second semester.

Learning to write well takes time. I will never forget the time I walked into a second-grade classroom where the teacher had just read *Twilight Comes Twice*, a lyrical picture book.

"We read your book *Twilight Comes Twice*," one boy told me. His eyes were shining. "You got beautiful language in that book."

This was an epiphany to me. In his own way this small boy was telling me: "Maybe I can't do it yet, maybe I can't write like you do, but I can hear it." And if he can hear it, he can one day do it himself. Powerful books build roads inside our students, paths they will eventually travel to create their own writing.

Teaching can be extremely isolating. One young teacher told me that on the first day of school the principal said: "Welcome to our school. Here's your classroom. I'll see you again in thirty years."

This tongue-in-cheek comment reveals a stubborn nugget of truth. Except for the occasional classroom visit or observation, teachers are largely left alone. Teaching writing can be particularly lonely. But when teachers offer their students powerful models—sometimes called "mentor texts"— we bring a new voice of authority in the classroom, giving students another source from which to learn. And it builds community when the teachers as well as the students share a wonderful text, marvel at it, and learn together as apprenticing writers.

A MENTOR LOOKS AT THE BIG PICTURE

All writers have off-days, get bored, get silly, get blocked, get derivative, get lazy, "borrow" sentences. It's important to remember to take the long view.

I learned an important idea about teaching writing while preparing for the birth of my son. In our childbirth class, our teacher had this suggestion for husbands (and writing teachers) who are nervous about doing and saying the right thing at the critical moment. Relax, she told us. Try to remember that *tenderness is more important than technique.*

Even the most skilled young writers can absorb only a certain amount of this fire, a limited amount of direct instruction, at any given time. We need to be patient: The fuse we light is a slow-burning one.

More important, we need to be gentle. Raymond Carver, writer and teacher, was revered by his students. The harshest criticism he would give to a student was: "I think it's good you got that story behind you."

Moments after my son Robert was born, his tight purple I-can't-be-lieve-this-is-happening-to-me face quickly dissolved into howls. A very loud howling indeed. I looked apprehensively at the midwife. She was smiling broadly.

"Do you see how strong his lungs and voice are?" she asked. "Remarkable!"

Minutes later Robert was being weighed. Next he had to take his first standardized test, the APGAR. I was astonished to see him hoist a tiny fist up to his mouth and begin sucking noisily.

"Look at that!" the midwife said, grinning. "Look at how well he's able to take care of himself!"

I looked at JoAnn. Amazing! It had *looked* like he was howling in distress. It had *seemed* like he was merely sucking his fists. But that midwife helped me to see it differently. And I expanded into the way she saw it. Strong lungs and voice. Yes, that's my robust little boy. Remarkable how he's able to take care of himself even as a tiny infant. I swelled with pride.

As a new father, I was wholly dependent on the midwife's appraisal of my newborn son. In the same way, young writers are deeply vulnerable to our appraisals of their stories, poems, or essays. We must speak to our students with an honesty tempered by compassion: Our words will literally define the ways they perceive themselves as writers.

Two

FREEZING TO THE FACE

Writing is easy. You just sit at the typewriter and open a vein.

—RED SMITH

I ONCE VISITED an art fair where one exhibit in particular caught my eye: a series of sculptures constructed entirely from automobile transmissions pulled from abandoned cars. The artist had twisted them into marvelously expressive shapes: a crane, a man, even an enormous double-humped camel. At the entrance to the exhibit a plaque was hanging (burnt letters in maple) that said: ART IS THE TRANSMISSION OF DISCOVERY.

Yes! And the saying seems just as applicable to the act of writing. Many people still assume that most writers bring a mental text that is more or less assembled when they encounter a blank piece of paper. Writing would seem to be merely a matter of transcribing onto paper what already exists in the mind. Right?

Wrong. Research on writing, and accounts from writers themselves, suggest a far stranger, far less logical writing process than that. Less neat. It turns out that many writers actually discover what they have to say in the process of writing it. The writer's challenge is to keep this sense of discovery intact; this keeps writing fresh and vibrant.

I discussed this notion of writing–as–discovery recently with a middle school teacher who insisted his students outline everything before they wrote it. He interrupted angrily.

"Are you kidding?" he asked. "Listen, let me ask you a question. Would you ever get on a bus if you didn't know where it was going? Would you?"

In such situations, I'm always torn between answering the rhetorical question or trying to address the hostility behind it. At that moment all I could do was stammer that writing and riding a bus are not the same thing and should not be approached as if they were identical.

But the more I thought about it the more it occurred to me that there is more than one way of riding a bus. True, riding a bus can be a simple matter of getting from here to there. But riding a bus (writing) can also be a way of *exploring* a new place (subject). Many times in Dublin, in Paris, or in the Caribbean, I boarded buses without knowing their exact destination. I simply rode around until I found a neighborhood that struck my fancy. A slice of the city was what I hungered for—that was the only *there* I was after. I still find this a terrific way of exploring a new place. In time you begin to notice landmarks, you begin to get a feel for the territory. You can always get off and get on a new bus anytime you feel like it.

Marilyn Jody, professor of English at Western Carolina University and an important mentor of mine, told me an anecdote about mountain climbing. While scaling a sheer rock face, mountain climbers face a dilemma that forces them to act in a way that is counter-intuitive and would seem to go against all common sense. For a moment, a mountain climber must let go of whatever perch he has secured to reach to the next higher place. There is no way around it. A climber who is too frightened to let go finds himself "frozen to the face," literally unable to move. He hangs there, paralyzed by fear. Finally, when his strength gives out, he falls.

It's hard not to see this story as a parable for many moments in life: loving, learning/teaching, and writing. Writers of all ages face myriad subtle temptations to "freeze to the face" by writing something safely mainstream and formulaic. F. Scott Fitzgerald and Raymond Chandler were both tempted by lucrative monetary contracts to write for the screen instead of writing novels. (Faulkner and Steinbeck did write screenplays and were extremely disappointed in the outcome.) The same thing often happens in classrooms. Students learn to find out what a teacher expects and write to those expectations—and the accompanying grades—instead of trying to internalize their own high standards for writing.

When I was twenty-one I sat down to write a novel. What did it matter that my life up to that point had been, as I freely admitted to myself, fairly unremarkable? My novelistic options seemed limited to three choices—college years, my family, and a half-serious love affair—all of which were still too recent to afford me the benefit of any real perspective or reflective wisdom. But I didn't know that, and I wouldn't have cared if I had known. I was determined to make my mark. I wanted to write a novel and concocted a plot suitable enough for this purpose.

I began by making a serious outline. This took nearly two weeks. Every chapter got outlined right down to the small a. and b. I wrote my novel the way I figured all writers wrote: by carefully following this outline. No matter what idea came into my head—a possible new complication, some unforeseen digression, or tantalizing character flaw—I pushed it aside if it did not appear on the original outline.

The result, of course, was disastrous: a stiff, lifeless work. Stillborn. I had frozen to the face of my outline and never allowed myself to take advantage of any startling little surprises that came up along the way. My novel was not a transmission of discovery because the outline did not allow for discovery, at least not the way I used it.

Books about the writing process and craft have helped demystify the act of writing. But maybe we need to *remystify* it. We have heard that clear writing comes from clear thinking. William Zinsser, among others, has exhorted us to write strong, uncluttered prose. Teachers of writing have worked hard to learn and teach the "writing logic" that would help students to write well. Skilled writing would seem to be similar to building a house. A writer needs material, a blueprint, and elbow grease to finish the project. Simple, isn't it?

But it's not that simple. When I write I am always struck by how complex, magical, illogical, and unexpected the process turns out to be. Take the writing of this book. For many months I gathered information in my accordion file on leads, endings, voice, sense of place, characterization. I assumed that these would become chapters in the book.

But when I began writing, the first chapter was called "Mentors," which was not one of the original sections in my accordion file. An aberration, perhaps. The next chapter, this one, had "Risk" as its working title. The chapter after that was titled "Words"; I was surprised to discover that I had a lot of ideas about that subject. None of these chapters were part of the book as I had originally conceived it. My book began evolving into something very different from what I'd imagined. The new chapters, less practical, more theoretical, confused me. What's going on? I wondered. Should I return to my original outline? I would have done so if this new material did not seem so absorbing. Compelled, if disoriented, I pushed ahead.

Do you know this story? A little girl watches a sculptor at work. He begins carving into a large wooden cube and works hard all day. By late

afternoon, the shape of a lion has begun to emerge. Absolutely dumbfound-
ed, the little girl looks at the sculptor and sputters, "But how did you know
there was a lion inside that wood?"

The writer experiences the same kind of childlike disbelief each time a
story/poem/novel/essay begins to take shape. And this is a major part of the
risk writers undertake—never knowing exactly what's going to turn up on
the page. Everything changes when you allow your writing to be influenced
and shaped by discoveries made during the process of writing. Your narrative is suddenly not as safe and predictable as you might have thought. You
swim across the river and find yourself far downstream of wherever it was
you hoped you'd end up. You discover that your topic has a hidden trapdoor
leading down into a dusty underbarn you would have preferred to stay out
of. You start writing about an antique table your grandmother owned, but
before you know it you are writing about the thrill and shame of a secret
romance you had with your first cousin, a girl who didn't look or seem the
least bit like a blood relative. You begin writing about getting your allowance
every Saturday morning and find yourself writing about that stack of new
twenty dollar bills you found when you were twelve years old under your
father's sweaters in the bottom drawer of his dresser. . . .

No, skilled writers don't meander off topic every chance they get. They
don't entertain every whim that comes into their heads. The writer must find
a middle ground between this kind of free writing and the rigid way I wrote
my first novel. A writer may find a creative tension springing up between the
original vision of the writing and how it turns out. But the temptation will
always exist to take the safe way out—to cling stubbornly to the cliff. Among
the many hidden traps a writer must circumnavigate, *success,* and the decep-
tive safety it seems to provide, may be the most insidious trap of all.

During college I spent a day helping a very old and retired obstetrician
plant five hundred pine saplings. I was touched by the quiet heroism of
this act—planting trees that would never grant him shade—and a few years
later I wrote a short story about it. I sent it off to *Redbook.* They promptly
accepted it, agreed to pay me $400, and published it in their Christmas edi-
tion. This success had a galvanizing effect on my shaky confidence: the cold
cash, the millions of readers, being published in the same issue as Ray Bradbury. On an airplane, in February, I met a young woman from Albuquerque
who had read the story and who flattered me with her praise. My spirits
soared. All of this was wonderful, except that now I was hooked. I wanted
to be a writer for *Redbook.* I wanted my stories to be smiled at by mothers
over their morning coffee in Albuquerque, Anchorage, Aspen, Atlanta. . . . I

wanted to be on the *inside* for a change. I had paid my dues, hadn't I? And for two years I tried to replicate this early success. I mailed a steady stream of stories to *Redbook*—all of them wholesome and poignant and awful. After *Redbook* rejected them, I sent them off to other magazines, and then to others. I began plastering rejection notices on the wall above my desk. It was not until five years later that I could clearly see how I'd frozen to this particular face: I had poisoned the voice in my writing by trying at all cost to be a popular magazine writer.

Students can fall into a similar trap, a trap set by us if we're not careful. We praise a student for trying an auditory lead ("Clomp! Clomp! Clomp! My brother thundered down the stairs . . ."). But now all of her writing begins with sound effects as she pursues additional praise.

In a sixth-grade classroom, I watched a boy try to work on a second draft of a story he had written. He sat slumped and dispirited while I tried to talk with him.

"Do you really want to do a second draft on this?" I asked. "Why don't you put it away and work on a new story?"

"I'd like to," he said, "but Mrs. C gave me a B⁻ on this first draft. She says if I work harder I can pull it up to an A⁻. I have to add more description and details. That's the kind of writing she likes."

This is one way we sabotage our students as risk takers. The cost runs high when we coerce students (through grades, praise, favoritism), however subtly, to shoehorn their emerging language into the narrow parameters we set for what constitutes "good writing" in our classrooms. As writing teachers, we need to ask ourselves some hard questions. How can we encourage students to internalize their own high standards for writing? Are we willing to allow these standards to differ from our own?

In Tom Robbins' wonderful novel *Even Cowgirls Get the Blues,* the author quips that "the only difference between a vacation and an adventure is the margin of safety." Writing is certainly no vacation. On many different levels, the writer faces a shaved margin of safety, if not outright danger: the danger of being misunderstood, ridiculed. The danger of failure. The danger of rejection. Years ago I had one poem rejected by an editor who wrote back: "Bad, bad, compares with your prose." I still have that rejection. It still hurts.

A writer becomes vulnerable by revealing part of her inner life. This is the fine print in the reader-writer agreement: When we read, we expect to learn about the writer and, through the writer, to learn about ourselves.

Writing with real honesty takes tremendous courage. Such writing should never be taken for granted; writers of all ages often find that they lack the nerve to write honestly. Factors of environment may figure into this—not simply the classroom environment but also the nefarious effects of television.

In *The Art of Fiction,* John Gardner says: "Much of the dialogue one encounters in student fiction, as well as plot, gesture, even setting, comes not from life but from life filtered through TV. Many student writers seem unable to tell their most important stories—the death of a father, the first disillusionment of love—except in terms of TV. And . . . TV is false to life."

Writing teachers cannot unplug students' TV sets, but we can watch for and celebrate the appearance of honest writing. In the poem in Figure 2-1, Jane, a third grader, speaks through the mask of being a penny. Jane uses an extended metaphor in a way that is very moving.

Brandon, a fourth grader, wrote the following poem "Adopted." Brandon's two metaphors follow hard upon each other, but the turbulence of the mixed metaphors helps to create the poem's undeniable power.

Adopted

I was almost like picked out of a hat. Being adopted feels something like that.
It's like going on a rollercoaster,
Landing with the wrong parents.

While visiting a school on Long Island, New York, I watched Francesca (a third grader) write this story:

HOW MY FAMILY CHANGED

My dad died when I was two months old. He died in a car accident. He was driving home from work. He was rushed to the hospital. By the time my mom got there the doctor told my mom he was dead. My mom told me all she could think about was me. How I would feel when I got older. One time my mom said: "You could have taken a bath in my tears, Francesca."

I don't feel great but I don't feel terrible that my father died. My mom is seeing someone who I was not crazy about at first. But now I like the man. His name is Joe. He is real nice. I decided to share my feelings with other children who have stories similar to mine so I joined a group called "Banana Splits." I feel so much better now that I know I can share my feelings with other kids. I can even talk with my mom. I love her.

Figure 2-1

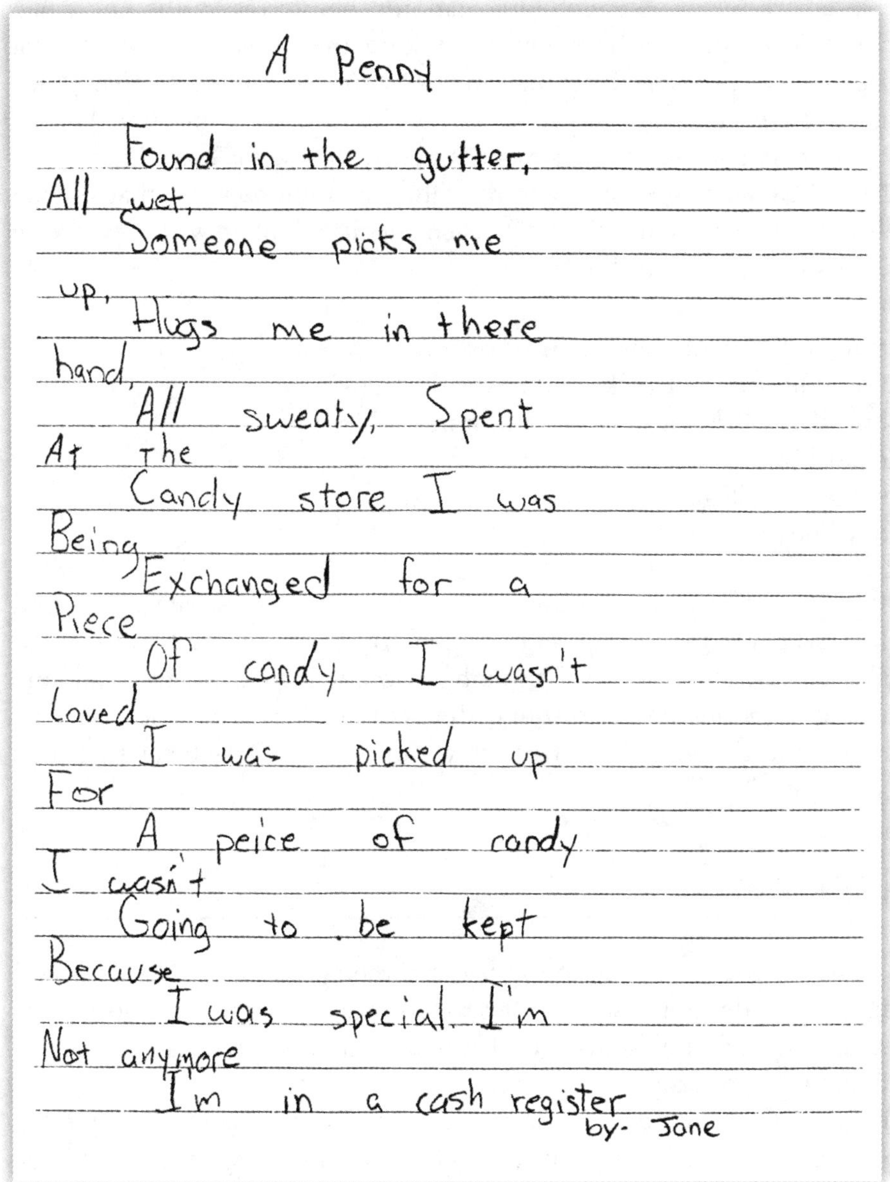

A Penny

Found in the gutter,
All wet,
Someone picks me
up,
Hugs me in there
hand,
All sweaty, Spent
At the
Candy store I was
Being
Exchanged for a
Piece
Of candy I wasn't
Loved
I was picked up
For
A peice of candy
I wasn't
Going to be kept
Because
I was special. I'm
Not anymore
I'm in a cash register

by- Jane

This young writer explores the most basic questions of all: Who am I? What is my history and how did it begin? As teachers we take a risk ourselves when we allow students to choose their own subjects, particularly when they decide to write about issues that make us uneasy.

The best writing classes I visit are taught by teachers who work hard to create an environment where children can put themselves on the line when they write. They do this by reading out loud the books and poems that powerfully affect them; students tune in to the emotion in their voices. They read accessible examples of literature that deal with risky issues (see Appendix). They share some of the resonant issues in their own lives. They write and share their writing—especially the false starts, the writing that doesn't work—with their students. When I teach writing, I often start by talking about ideas I might write about:

- Getting lost at the circus when I was seven
- Haunted house (on Block Island, Rhode Island)
- "Third Parent": being the oldest of nine children
- The last kiss
- Leaving for college
- Bobby's death

I find it helpful to divide this list into two categories: safe topics and risky topics. I suspect I could skate through fairly safe topics such as "haunted house" and "lost at the circus," though I would not expect to make any big discoveries about myself through the writing. I would rather take my chances on the thinner, though possibly richer, ice of a subject that feels more unresolved.

THE LAST KISS

If it had nothing else, my childhood had symmetry. Teeth brushed morning and night. Good deeds and sin. The bus to school and the bus back home. My mother and my father. Chores and play, light and dark, inside and out. Ale's Woods and the mowed grass of our lawn.

This symmetry seemed pervasive, an apparent law of nature. It extended to the kisses I got from my parents just before bed. First, my mother. At bedtime I would come to where she stood washing dishes, wiping the table, or, rarely, resting on the couch with her feet up.

"My poor dogs are barking," she'd sigh, smiling and leaning forward. To me, at least, our kisses were passionate moments that passed much too quickly. I was the oldest. She was the first woman I ever loved. A goodnight kiss from my mother meant a great big hug, as well; I learned that this was one way to extend the experience. Her cheek was smooth and soft. I walked away with the good, honest, hardworking smell of my mother's skin—along with the faint cigarette smokiness of her hair—in my nostrils.

All this happened in a matter of seconds. My mother's kisses contained potent medicine to ward off spirits of the night, but not potent enough. I was grateful to go next to my father. His goodnight kisses were more formal affairs, but that was all right. Formality was exactly what I wanted just before bed. And no accompanying body hug, either. Just this: his male scent, the faintest remnants of morning aftershave lotion, and the whisker-stubbly contour of his proffered cheek—a textured surface that made a satisfying contrast with my mother's cheek. Kissing my tall, handsome father always imbued me with a strong dose of masculine courage. Thus blessed, twice-kissed, I could go off safely to bed.

This arrangement worked very well indeed and lasted through kinder-garten, first grade, and into second grade. It was such an intrinsic part of my childhood—like making my bed or saying my prayers—that I never both-ered to question it.

One night I went to kiss my mother goodnight. Mom was bottle-feeding the eternal Fletcher baby (Joey? Kathy?) at the time; I had to lean over the little one to get to my mother. She let the baby cradle on her lap while she kissed and hugged me. It was from embraces like this one that I would learn a first crucial rule of affection: Important kisses always take place with the eyes closed. In my case, the better to feel her strong arms, her warmth. The better to concentrate on her smell: perfume, dishwashing lotion, and the smell that was simply her.

Next I went to find my father. He was working down in the basement; he glanced up at me when I approached. My father knew exactly why I was there, but on this evening he became busy and commenced to energetically beat the dust out of some window screens with a whisk broom. I watched him for a while, tapping my foot, trying to be patient. Several minutes passed.

"I'm going to bed, Dad," I said at last.

"Well, good night, then," he said, giving me a kind of half-smile, half-sigh that was peculiar to him. I was stunned. There was something in his voice that made me decide not to say it again.

I went to bed. Outside, sounds of the summer night: crickets, a sprinkler hissing, some neighborhood kids still playing, the ice-cream truck taunting kids with its twilight ringing.

Next night I decided to try my father again. Maybe last night's missed kiss was no more than a quirk. I went to him first this time and found him outside, behind his car, the trunk opened, sorting through book samples he would need to make his sales call the next day. He was on the road a great deal; it was not unusual for him to be gone all week. It was nearly 8:30 and the lawn behind him was alive with fireflies. They drifted through the cool twilight like bits of phosphorescent jellyfish in the tide. I approached him noisily, clearing my throat, shuffling my feet.

"It's bedtime," I murmured. I wonder, now, if he heard only those words or also the plea behind it, the desire for clarification. Maybe it was no more than the sound of quiet expectancy a child makes when he says: "I'm hungry." I don't know. I merely watched with a sinking heart as my father's hands got busy again, not with me but with something else, this time stacking his book samples in cardboard boxes. He stood up and turned to me. He reached forward to touch my arm. He squeezed my shoulder.

"Good night, then," he said, turning away. I stood there a moment, while the fireflies pulsed in silence. I was eight years old. The thought my mind held was too large to formulate into a question, too vague to clearly recognize as loss.

It took several more nights, several more awkward tries, before the grim truth finally sunk in. I was too old to be kissed by my father. True, I could go to my mother and get a huge bear hug along with a kiss. But now that the smoothness of her cheek was not counterbalanced by my father's fine sandpaper, even her kisses felt different, not nearly so powerful, much more fragile. I would never again embrace her without some part of me wondering if I might not one day lose her kisses, as well.

Three

A LOVE OF WORDS

Language permits us to see.
Without the word, we are all blind.

—CARLOS FUENTES, *The Old Gringo*

STRANGE OCCURRENCES. One fall day I took a group of kids to the Bronx Zoo. We reached the buffaloes and stopped to admire the immense bulk, the shaggy shredding coats.

"Buffaloes!" a little boy said, and I felt a stab of pure emotion, sharp, bittersweet.

"C'mon, let's go," another kid said. But I couldn't move. Buffaloes. The word reverberated oddly inside my head. I was dazed, rooted to the spot. I was actually on the brink of tears. Yet I couldn't quite bring it to the surface, that deep memory fragment. I shook it off and all but forgot it.

On the way home from the zoo the kids started singing "Home on the Range," and when they got to the part "where the buffaloes roam" there it was again—pungent emotion, pure and sad and sweet, surging up inside me.

Months passed. One day I was hanging up JoAnn's white bathrobe and just like that the memory came flooding back. Dad's bathrobe. When I was little, for some reason (the shaggy bulk?) we always called Dad's bathrobe his "buffalo." He traveled a lot during those years, selling books all over New England. The first thing he did when he came home on Friday night was to don slippers and that big white terrycloth bathrobe. We would snuggle hard against that buffalo while he read stories to us before bed.

Some nights during the week while Dad was away we would start pestering my mother. Couldn't we take Dad's buffalo out of his closet? Just for a little while? If she agreed, we'd race upstairs to the closet in his bedroom. The buffalo always hung on a particular hook; we would jostle each other to be first to pull it down. The buffalo got dragged downstairs to the living room where we would wrap it around us while we watched TV. It was so big that two or even three kids could nestle within its white bulk. Beyond its warmth and softness, the most wonderful thing about the robe was how it had soaked up Dad's essence, his *smell*. We would sit there, wrapped in the warmth and comforting scent of the father we missed so much. I discovered that if I closed my eyes it was nearly possible to believe that he really was there himself, holding us in his strong arms.

Today the word *buffalo* sounds to me like power commingled with regret: the mighty beasts that were all but wiped out as white America moved west. But it also holds a deeper and more personal regret tangled up with missing my father.

~

Artists develop a love for the feel of their tools, the smell and texture of clay, wood, or paint. My brother Jim has imported ebony all the way from Nigeria for some of his most memorable sculptures. The lithographer Tanya Grosman searched the world to find paper of astonishing beauty and rarity to lure artists such as Jasper Johns, Larry Rivers, Buckminster Fuller, and Robert Rauschenburg to her Universal Limited Art Editions studio in West Islip, New York.

Writers are no different. Writers love words. And while writers occasionally get excited over new voice-recognition software or other high-tech gizmo, words remain the most important tool a writer has to work with.

"If you want to write and you're not in love with your language, you shouldn't be writing," Jane Yolen says bluntly. "Words are the writer's tools."

"When I write," Cynthia Rylant says, "my mind's not filled with visual imagery. It's filled with language. Words. I seek words, I chase after them. When I write I'm trying to put the most beautiful words in the world down on paper."

Not all writers work like Rylant; some writers do begin with images, others with emotion. Either way the writer must use words to communicate the story/image/emotion. Writers obsess over words, their origins and their sounds. Writers have pet words, favorite and worst words, words imbued with other associations and personal meanings. In *One Writer's Beginnings,* Eudora Welty describes the sensual awareness she developed of particular words such as moon: "The word 'moon' comes into my mouth as though fed to me out of a silver spoon. Held in my mouth the moon became a word. It had the roundness of a Concord grape Grandpa took off his vine and gave me to suck out of its skin and swallow whole, in Ohio."

Writers love their language, but the language they love may not be a conventional tongue. Mark Twain's many books captured the colorful vernacular of the Mississippi region. Eloise Greenfield is one of many African-American writers to use Black English for her sparkling book of poems, *Honey, I Love.* And Darrell H. Y. Lum, a Hawaiian writer, uses a rich and musical pidgin English in his short story "The Moiliili Bag Man." The language used by a writer may be powerful or lyrically beautiful even when it does not conform to conventional grammar.

A writer's fascination with words has roots in a child's natural tendency to play with language.

> GRACIE (3 years old): Mom, do I talk a lot?
>
> MOM: Yes, you're very talkative!
>
> GRACIE: Is Mugsy (the family dog) talkative?
>
> MOM: No, not really.
>
> GRACIE (giggling): Right, he's barkative!

"Read like a wolf eats," Gary Paulsen advises young readers, and as a boy I did just that. I was a ravenous reader, and it didn't take long to figure out that each new word brought me into a whole new room, with new views and distinct intellectual furniture. The Boy Scout Oath's lofty aims ("trustworthy, loyal, helpful, friendly, courteous, kind, obedient, cheerful, thrifty, brave, clean, and reverent") were counterbalanced by less pure descriptors such as *voluptuous* and *callipygian*—exotic and barely understood words I first encountered in books, words that took on sultry new nuances as I moved into adolescence.

One sweltering summer day, while my young father struggled to cut the lawn with a hand mower, I was sitting with my best friend on the porch. He confided to me the worst swear in the world. Only nine years old, I watched from a safe distance my father mop sweat off his forehead while my friend whispered the muggy monosyllabic word, softly, so my father would not hear. It seemed monstrous that such a word could coexist juxtaposed (another of my favorite words) against the image of my saintly, toiling father. Swears amazed me. "Duck" was perfectly all right, but if your mother heard you rhyme that word with another word only two letters after the "D" you could get your mouth washed out with soap.

Another amazing thing: Words could mean different things at different times. The spoken word "see" might also mean "sea"—or even the letter "c." Many words contained delightful shades of ambiguity. When I was five I loved to play with homonyms: "bear" and "bare," "red" and "read." This early language play would later blossom in a poem like "Waves" (from *Water Planet*):

> *Waves on the ocean,*
> *Ripples on the sand,*
> *My father calling me*
> *With a wave of his hand.*
>
> *The wavy grain of wood,*
> *The wave in my hair,*
> *Waves of fiery autumn leaves*
> *Tumbling through the air.*
>
> *A wave of sadness*
> *When I think of the way*
> *My best friend Vinnie*
> *Moved far far away.*

I grew up in Brant Rock, Massachusetts, where there was a fabulous candy store: Buds. Once a week, if we were lucky, my mother would walk us down to Buds, where the bins and counters were crammed with chocolate cigarettes and bubblegum cigars, red wax lips and black wax mustaches, dots and red hots, jawbreakers and ju-ju beads. . . . Many of the candies were priced two or even three for a penny; if you shopped wisely you could end up with a whole bag of sweets for a nickel or a dime.

At that time *bamboozled* and *flabbergasted* were my favorite words. I loved the feel of those words in my mouth, and still cannot conjure them up except in terms of taste. *Bamboozled* has a fizzly Sweet Tart taste that begins in a rush of sweetness but always ends with a tingly, tickly feeling at the top of the mouth. *Flabbergasted,* on the other hand, tastes and sounds as nutty as a Heath Bar.

In my writer's notebook I keep lists of favorite words, some of which I love for the odd pictures they make in my mind, others merely for their exotic sounds: *babushka, cockatoo, pumpernickel,* and *periwinkle.* In high school I traded words with similarly inclined friends. (We were not necessarily the most popular kids in school.) Each word carried its own peculiar kind of melody. While words like *umber, mellow, sonorous,* and *quiescent* sounded sooth-ing, *obstreperous, truculent, vituperative,* and *obdurate* seemed to jut their very chins out at the world.

The Fletcher family was a den of rabid Boston Bruins hockey fans. The Bruins had a few future Hall of Fame players, like Phil Esposito and Bobby Orr, plus a bunch of guys who were adept at fighting. The Bruins were forever getting into brawls. I was an avid reader of the *Boston Globe* sports section, and it was great fun trying to envision the sports writers thumbing through their thesauruses in search of new words for these nightly alterca-tions. My siblings and I roared over the words they came up with: *imbroglio, fisticuffs, melee, slugfest, donnybrook,* and (my favorite) *brouhaha.*

In high school, while other kids admired teachers with the best looks, biggest muscles, or fastest cars, I admired those teachers with the most re-markable vocabularies. Mr. Thompson and Mr. Plumer were able to take words like *perspicacious* and *contemporaneous* and weave them seamlessly into their lectures. I would copy down the words and race home to look them up.

I discovered that by placing two ordinary words next to each other, you could wake them up and create an effect that went far beyond the reach of either one. This is what led me to title my first book *Walking Trees,* taken from a conversation I had with a first-grade girl. Put together, these two words try to pull each other in opposite directions. The phrase *walking trees* embodies a concept almost impossible to put in words: paradox, when two opposing ideas can both be true at the same time.

In the early 1960s, my siblings and I roamed the thick pine woods around our house in Marshfield, Massachusetts. My brother Jim was a born natural-ist, with vacuum eyes that sucked up incredible treasures during his long soli-tary treks through the woods. Every day he would bring home some unusual insect, snake, or turtle he had found.

One day, after a bad windstorm, Jim and I were walking through a swampy part of the woods. A tree had fallen in the storm and a shallow pool had formed in the crater left by the huge mass of uplifted roots. We saw something lurch into the edge of the water, a kind of lizard we had never seen before. We got just the briefest glimpse of red before the creature disappeared.

"Didya see that?"

"It looked like some kind of newt," I said. "A salamander."

"That was no salamander," Jim said. "Didn't you see the red on its gills?"

Jim went home and proceeded to pull out several volumes of the World Book Encyclopedia. For two hours he sat poring through volumes A (am-phibians), L (lizard), and R (reptiles).

"I found it," he said, showing me a picture. "A mud puppy. That's definitely it. We saw a mud puppy. They're common around here, found in the swamps, rivers, and lakes of northeastern America. Their external gills are bright red."

Mud puppy! I fell in love with the odd name, the internal rhyme, the funny image it forced into my head. The name clicked. By the end of that week all the kids in the neighborhood were calling the swampy area near that uprooted tree Mud Puppy Place.

Words are a writer's primal tools but anyone who tries to write English—child or adult—immediately gets caught in a kind of linguistic stranglehold that makes it difficult to use those tools. The English language contains about 490,000 words, along with another 300,000 technical terms.[*] No one, of course, not even the great writers, can utilize so much richness. It has been said that Shakespeare had a working vocabulary of around 33,000 words. In 1945, the average American student between the ages of six and fourteen had a written vocabulary of 25,000 words. Today, that vocabulary has shrunk to about 10,000 words.

The mass media has helped to further tighten this noose. Popular print media draw from a small group of words; television, of course, draws from the smallest pool of all. The implications for the shrinking population of words go far beyond the dangers of falling SAT scores.

It seems to me that the first step toward addressing this problem is for teachers to model their own curiosity with words. Recently I decided to bring a bag of words into the schools where I work as a writing consultant. I wanted to let kids know how crucial words are to me as a writer. But how to proceed? I was surer about what I *didn't* want to do. I knew I didn't want to turn it into a vocabulary lesson, carefully disguised instruction on roots or suffixes, or an exercise in using the dictionary.

I walked into a fifth-grade classroom and began by writing some of my favorite words on the board. Some were funny sounding words: *persnickety, oxymoron,* and *troglodyte* (which the students immediately seized upon for its usefulness in insulting people). I had also chosen several small words for their sheer potency: *triage, quisling, quietas.*

Kids started scrambling for the dictionaries. It turned out, however, that the school-use dictionaries in the classroom didn't house most of the words

---

[*] There are varying estimates for the size of the English language. The editors of *Webster's Third New International Dictionary, Unabridged* include 475,000 main headwords, but in their preface they estimate the true number to be much higher.

I had brought in with me. I sent a student down to the library. A few minutes later he returned, grunting under the weight of Webster's monstrous 2,347-page, 320,000-word *New Universal Unabridged Dictionary.* We were in business.

Mnemonic. Touchstone. Onomatopoeia. The kids were delighted to learn that *fontanel* is the word for the soft spot at the top of a baby's head. Next, I scribbled on the board several truly bizarre words:

> *jirble*—a craving for unnatural food, such as dust
> *geniophobia*—fear of chins
> *xenoglossy*—understanding a language one has never learned

"Probably the longest word in the English language is *pneumonoultramicroscopicsilicovolcanoconiosis,*" I told the students. "Forty-five letters. It's a kind of lung disease miners can get."

The kids howled, impressed that I knew what it meant and could actually pronounce it. They asked me to say it several more times and insisted I print it on the board.

"How about you?" I asked. "Do you have any favorite words?"

"I've always liked *plummet,*" one boy said. "I like the way it sounds."

"I like *tintinnabulation,*" one girl said, pronouncing the word perfectly. "It means the ringing of bells."

I wrote down their words: *déjà vu, exposé, deciduous.*

"I like the word *mistress,*" one very tall girl said. "I mean, I don't like what it means but I like how it sounds." She paused and looked at me with narrowed eyes. "What *does* it mean?"

I glanced at the fifth-grade teacher. The teacher answered immediately, as if she had been expecting the question.

"*Mistress* is one of those words with more than one meaning," she explained. "Mistress can be a proper title for a woman. And it can also be the word for a woman who goes out with a married man."

"Oh," the girl said.

Jane Yolen describes three different vocabularies: a reading vocabulary, a writing vocabulary, and a speaking vocabulary. "There are some words that are wonderful but they're reading words only, or writing words—not speaking words," Yolen says. "And those of us who are writers also have a secret vocabulary."

My secret vocabulary includes words I often save for a long time, several years, until I can actually use them in a piece of writing. I hoarded *postprandial* (an adjective meaning "after dinner," as in "postprandial coffee") for no less than five years and was thrilled to actually be able to use the word in my first book. Another secret word of mine is *gegenschein*—a faint, glowing spot in the sky exactly opposite the position of the sun; also called "counterglow." I have kept this word for a long, long time; I'm not at all sure I shall ever find a legitimate place to use it in a sentence. Still, it's great to have such a word around in case the need arises.

A rich vocabulary allows a writer to get a richness of thought onto the paper. However, the writer's real pleasure comes not from using an exotic word but from using the *right* word in a sentence. Once, while writing an article, I labored over this sentence: "Many school districts are finding it difficult to _____ balanced literacy with a culture that values numerical data from testing above all else."

I could not think of the missing word. But I knew it was out there—the single word that would make the sentence click, make its meaning snap into instant focus. It had something to do with paradox, with linking two things that don't quite go together. *Juxtapose* was close, but it wasn't the right word. I kept plugging other, less precise words into the sentence and rereading to see how it sounded. *Link? No. Equate?* No. *Compare? Bridge?* Nope. Finally, I gave up and moved to another part of the article.

That night, in bed, I suddenly opened my eyes and sat bolt upright.

"*RECONCILE!*" I said to JoAnn.

"Huh?"

"*Reconcile!*" I grinned at her. "The word I've been looking for. 'School districts are finding it difficult to *reconcile* balanced literacy with a culture that values numerical data from testing above all else.' Eureka!"

As teachers, we can share with students the pleasure in finding the precise word to communicate a nuance of thought. We can encourage students to play with language. And we can celebrate their language breakthroughs wherever and whenever they occur. After reading *Charlotte's Web*, Donna, a third grader, told her teacher: "I think I want to use the word *perish* in my story instead of *die*."

Is *perish* a better word than *die*? Not necessarily. Not always. Often a simple word is better than the fancy word. But in this case Donna took a big risk: She moved a word from her reading vocabulary to her writing vocabulary, a word she had never before used in a piece of writing. That's what I mean by a language breakthrough.

In the Bronx, Denton, a first grader, wrote the story shown in Figure 3-1.

Figure 3-1

Where had Denton come upon *beloved,* an old-fashioned word that intermingles love, respect, and a kind of religious reverence?

"It's a wonderful piece of writing," I told Denton. "That word *beloved* makes it even more special to read."

PLAYING WITH WORDS

Not only do writers love words, they cherish the opportunity to play with them. In this regard, writers are building off the language play we see in small children from the moment they begin to talk. Sara, a Canadian teacher who is also a single mother, told me this story about her four-year-old daughter, Anwyn.

> *Anwyn has seen me at the kitchen table, surrounded by papers, my computer and looking exhausted. She knows that every night I mark papers and that my least favorite time of the year is doing report cards. Recently I crawled into bed at 3 am to find her sleeping in it. She opened her eyes and said: "What! You're only coming to bed now? I never want to be a teacher!" When I asked her why, she said "Marking" and fell asleep. Later that week, she told me she knew who my boyfriend was. I was stunned and asked, "Who?" and she replied, "Mark Reports." Since then she jokes how I am always spending too much time with Mark Reports, and that we should just throw him in the fire. In mid-June Anwyn said, "Now that it's summer I guess you and Mark Reports will be taking a break from each other, huh?"*

Strong writing contains an element of surprise, which is an intrinsic part of wordplay. Writers boldly invent new words: *splendiferous, chillax,* and *cyberspace* (invented by William Gibson in his novel *Neuromancer,* 1984). They twist words, stretch them, link them in outlandish ways, and tease out new meanings. They revel in hyperbole, humorous expressions, and rhetorical flourishes: "We may have come over to America on different ships, but we're all in the same boat now." (Whitney Young, Jr.) They jump at the chance to use a pun, especially in a book title, as with *Miss Alaineus: A Vocabulary Disaster* by Debra Frasier.

Nowadays wordplay has fallen upon hard times in the classroom. In recent years I have observed a persistent push to sanitize the content of student writing. As I go from school to school I'm disheartened to find more and more formulaic writing, prose where all quirks and surprises have been carefully removed. This does not reflect my concept of strong writing. I believe that as writers it is our responsibility to keep language fresh, to summon up its supple power every time we sit down to write. I want to see more playful writing because that's the kind of writing that makes you want to sit up, laugh, pay attention.

Wordplay might seem like a frivolous activity reserved for extremely clever people. In fact, it's a powerful tool. At my sister's wedding, my eighty-year-old father got up to speak. He wanted to share a few words about what can happen when you meet your soul mate.

"My life growing up wasn't so wonderful," Ralph Sr. admitted. "It was like the beginning of *The Wizard of Oz,* when everything is in black and white. You know the moment when that movie switches to color? Well, when I met my beloved wife Jean my life switched to color. I had 52 years of brilliant Technicolor. But when she died, my life went back to black and white."

As he spoke these words, I looked down the pew and caught every one of my siblings (including me) wiping tears from our eyes. My father used two kinds of wordplay: he made an allusion to a well-known film, and he used a metaphor (his life turned from color to black and white). He didn't do this to be clever or to show how smart he was. Rather, he used wordplay because it was the most powerful way to express what he wanted to convey.

There's one more vocabulary I hoard. This one has less to do with exotic words than with words saturated in strong memories. A word like *buffalo* contains potent medicine; its music conjures up an entire era of my life. I think of it as a "trapdoor" word. Its conventional meaning hides a secret trapdoor that leads down to an unexpected or previously forgotten layer of memory underneath. The mere mention of such a word is enough to bring it all back in a flood.

Take the word *sheriff.* This serious word has been altered forever by the association I have with Valerie Sheriff, a girl on whom I had a hopeless crush during eleventh and twelfth grades. She was stunning, and she was in the classes with all the smartest kids, which only intensified the awe in which I held her. Today I cannot watch a western with outlaws and sheriffs without immediately thinking of Valerie Sheriff, her straight blond hair and flawless features, the cool California air about her, the impossibly long legs beneath her cheerleader miniskirt, the energetic splits she did on the sidelines during football games that always left me feeling weak.

Or take *elegant.* My grandmother, Annie Collins, came from Arlington, Massachusetts, each year to spend Christmas with our family in New York. At our Christmas Eve dinner, Grandma Annie, Aunt Mary, my parents, and all seven or eight or nine kids would be sitting around the big table with the best plates and silverware, the food heaped high, a glass of red wine for the grownups, even a thimbleful for the kids. After the food was served, and grace said, everyone paused. We kids had to wait, drooling over our drumsticks, mouths watering over mounds of butternut squash with molten craters of butter on top. It was traditional that before the rest of us could dig in, Grandma Annie had to be the first one to take a mouthful of turkey.

"Oh, Jean, this is *elegant,*" she would say. That set everything into motion. Now Mom could blush her thanks, everyone else could laugh, and we could all start eating. But we knew. Young as we were, we understood some of the significance of that word spoken here in New York by our Bostonian grandmother, a word that seemed to rhyme with "delicate," a word that carried its nostalgic ring of old Boston, maybe more civilized times, legends of Ted Williams and Jack Kennedy, the times she marched on the Boston Common as a suffragette, and the night she danced with "Honey" Fitz at an office party in Filene's Basement where she worked.

Grandma Annie died at the age of ninety-two. Today, in my family, the word *elegant* still gets spoken around the holidays, and always with a great deal of reverence.

PART **TWO**

The Craft

Four

THE ART OF SPECIFICITY

Keep listening. Keep your radar out. Take everything,
because it is matter for your work.
No detail is too small.

—MARY TALLMOUNTAIN

A **FRIEND** of mine broke up with his girlfriend. She seemed like a terrific person, bright and energetic. I asked him why.

"Lots of reasons," he said to me. "For one thing, she was eating too high off the food chain."

Ha! This remark—which still strikes me as hilarious—got carefully tucked away in my writer's notebook. I just knew that someday I would find a place for it in my writing: in a story, poem, or book.

A few years later I found myself teaching a college writing course. My students wrote with gusto; they wrote a great deal. If their writing had any generic weakness, it was the lack of specifics needed to substantiate points made in the text.

"You've got to get more specific," I said to the students during one class. "You're way too general. You can't expect readers to eat too high off the food chain."

Some people laughed—myself included. But later, in a more sober moment, I decided that I actually liked the point I had made and even the way I had made it. In any piece of writing there is a kind of food chain, a continuum of thought ranging from the most general (nostalgia, Oedipal love, failed dreams) to the most concrete (burnt paper, a cat's sandpapery tongue, dead leaves scrape-dancing across a sidewalk). Readers are omnivorous: they nourish themselves on the entire food chain. Still, each element on the chain depends on the element below it. Ultimately, as Donald Murray pointed out, "readers are bottom feeders." Writing needs to be grounded in plenty of physical details. Without them the whole food chain falls apart.

As a boy I suffered from hay fever. Not just ragweed or goldenrod but also common grass right around mid-spring. When I rolled or wrestled in the grass my eyes would commence itching, whereupon I'd rub them, my hands now invisibly gloved in grass pollen. The itch would intensify. This prompted me to rub more vigorously still. Some afternoons would find my eyes nearly swollen shut.

Only my mother knew how to interrupt this cycle before I succeeded in tearing my eyes from their sockets. She'd bring me into the house, make me lie down, and put over my eyes a face cloth that had been soaked in cold water and folded into an inch and a half strip.

This helped. Pressed gently down, the wet cloth soothed those tortured orbs. And being deprived of my sight every day for forty-five minutes at a time taught me to pay attention to sounds and smells I had never before noticed. I heard my little brothers singing one of their silly songs outside the window:

Mary, Mary, long before the fashions came,

With her head chopped off and her belly, too,

She looked so much like a moo . . .

Lying in darkness on the couch, I learned to distinguish whoever was coming down the stairs by the sound of their footsteps. Not just Mom and Dad—that was easy—but also Jim or Elaine, Tom, or Bob.

I listened to baseball. Only in total darkness could I fully picture those Red Sox games. Now the players came to life—not just their stats and quirks but also their exotic names. Pumpsie Green. Félix Mantilla. Bill Monbouquette. Some afternoons I would lie in blissful darkness and repeat that name—Bill Monbouquette (who was a great bunter for a pitcher, by the way)—fifty or sixty times.

And smells. The impossibly sweet spring air. The aroma of freshly mowed grass, which entranced me even as it wreaked additional havoc on my allergies. The many different bodily odors soaked into the couch. A panoply of smoke smells I learned to differentiate: cigarette smoke (my mother), smoke from something frying on the stove (onions), and smoke from outside (someone in the neighborhood burning trash in their backyard incinerator).

BEAUTIFUL WRITING

Every writing teacher has at one time or another exhorted students: Get specific! I want to see concrete details! Pay closer attention to the particular! This suggests the irresistible argument for encouraging students to begin by writing from their own experience. Don Murray reminded us that effective writing begins with "honest, specific, accurate" information. When students write from experience, they can breathe those specifics into their writing— dialect, odd smells, precise names of plants—that can animate even the most tired and tedious text. The following narrative, by a fourth grader, begins with a distant, neutral tone as she lists her family's moves from town to town. But when the author slows down and goes under the surface, delving into the specifics, the effect is startling.

> MY LIFE CHANGED
>
> When my parents got married they lived in the Bronx. Then they moved to Seaford. And that's when they had me. Three years later my parents had my sister. We were just moving out of Seaford. Then we moved to Merrick. And that's when something terrible happened. One year later when I was five and my sister was two, we were sleeping in my mom and dad's room. And then in the middle of the night, my dad got dressed, took some food and money, his briefcase for work, and just walked out. For some reason mom and dad always seemed to yell at each other. My only prayers and dreams are for them to get back together.

Those common household objects—food, money, briefcase—reverberate in the mind's eye and give a terrible concreteness to the father's departure.

I spent several days working with Dr. Linda Wells and a group of sixth-grade teachers in East Williston, New York. We were noticing that much of the student writing in those classes tended to be very literal, flat.

"When I talk about details with young writers," Linda Wells said, "I spend time talking about what a visual image is."

"It's funny," one teacher said, "because we've spent lots of time reading and rereading books with rich language, like *Owl Moon* (Jane Yolen). We read *I'm in Charge of Celebrations* (Byrd Baylor) and talked about the imagery. Those books are so beautiful, and the kids really loved them, but so far it hasn't had much effect on their writing."

"Wait a moment," I said. "Are we talking about *beautiful* writing or are we talking about *specific* writing?"

"That's just it," Linda said. "The writing becomes beautiful when it becomes specific, concrete."

The writing becomes beautiful when it becomes specific. That remark haunted me. I wrote it down. Thought about it. During the weeks that followed I began to suspect that Linda was right. In a sixth-grade class one boy wrote: "When I was a baby, I used to drag around this blanket. You couldn't pry it away from me. At night, I'd chew on the threads and they'd get caught in my teeth, like dental floss. My mother used to wait until I was asleep until she could reach into my mouth and try to pull out the threads."

The class laughed appreciatively at these quirky details. Another boy in the same class wrote: "When I was little, I used to take a silk scarf to bed with me. When my dad would kiss me goodnight, his eyebrow would brush the top of my forehead. I loved the way that felt. After he left and turned out the light, I'd take out the scarf. I found that if I rubbed the scarf with one hand, and my own eyebrow with the other, it would feel exactly like my father's eyebrow."

There is nothing exceptional in the words these writers use: blanket, dental floss, eyebrows, silk. The power comes from the details and the absolute authority they lend to those early childhood memories, lovingly excavated and displayed before us. The writing becomes beautiful when it becomes specific.

I delighted in this poem by Lindsay, a third grader.

Eyes

Eyes are special things.
They are slammed on your face
when you are born.
Eyes are what you see poems with
and watch the world turn around and around.
   If you did not have eyes
you would not see your puppy slide across the porch
when it's raining.

This writer knows how to *see*. In a single stroke she uses a few simple details, clearly observed, to create an ending of breathtaking clarity.

HOW SMALL DETAILS CAN EVOKE BIG ISSUES

I wrote a feature article for *People* magazine about the late Dr. Joseph Panzarella, a quadriplegic doctor who may be the single most remarkable individual I ever met. Multiple sclerosis had left him without the use of his hands or legs. He needed an assistant to dress and feed him. A special hydraulic lift mounted on top of his car hoisted him to and from his wheelchair. Still, he managed to be medical director of a large rehabilitation hospital, the father of seven children, and author of a remarkable memoir, *Spirit Makes a Man*.

Panzarella and his wife, Josephine, were devoted to each other. But in the article I didn't want to use that cliché: "devoted couple." I began looking for some example, some anecdote or detail from their life to illustrate the depth of their interconnectedness. One day Panzarella told me:

"Did you know that every night my wife wakes up every two hours and turns me in bed?" He smiled. "Otherwise I'd get bed sores. I can't turn myself. Can you imagine? She's been turning me every two hours, every night, for the past fifteen years. She's some kind of woman."

I made sure to include that detail in the article.

A few years later I took a writing course from novelist Richard Price.

"The bigger the issue, the smaller you write," Price said one day in class. "Remember that. You don't write about the horrors of war. No. You write about a kid's burnt socks lying on the road. There's this science fiction story where a guy comes back from space and finds that everyone on earth is dead from a nuclear war. He just drives around for a couple of days. But here's the thing: Even though he's the only one left, he still finds himself stopping for traffic signs, traffic lights. He can't help it. That's what you do. You pick the smallest manageable part of the big thing, and you work off the resonance."

The bigger the issue, the smaller you write. Very smart advice: possibly the single most important suggestion you will find in this book. It is the kind of insight that has taken me years to fully appreciate.

Recently I asked a high school teacher if there was a drug problem in his school. He smiled sadly, shook his head.

"Not really, not now, but let me tell you about something that happened a couple years ago. One of our students got hurt on the athletic field. Broke his leg in three places. They had to bring in a helicopter and pull the kid out. The big copter landed right on the field. When kids saw the helicopter, they panicked. 'The narcs are coming! The narcs are coming.' They rushed out

Figure 4-1

I love you mom and I know you do too and always will, too. And I do too, mom. My mom liked to sing and when her voice got quieter I sang for her. She liked to collect cute things. And I gave her (grave) stone a cute snowman. But mom can still hear me. My mom is singing in the picture.

of their classes and into the bathroom. All you could hear was the sound of toilets flushing and flushing all over the school."

The story in Figure 4-1 was written by Katie, a first grader whose mother had died two years earlier. Nearly every piece of writing she completed that year had something to do with this tragic event.

The bigger the issue, the smaller you write. You don't write about a serious drug problem. You write about a helicopter landing and the sound of toilets flushing frantically throughout a high school. You don't write about the death of a mother. You write about how "her voice got quieter."

The writers whose work is cited in this chapter are not afraid to let their readers get close to the raw materials of their stories. They trust that, given enough specifics, enough information, the reader is wholly capable of making the leap from the concrete to the larger issue.

Concrete details allow the writer to *understate* an important truth rather than clubbing the reader over the head with it. Such details have an uncanny way of getting to the heart of complex issues, making further explanations unnecessary.

THE RECURRING DETAIL

Freud pointed out that as human beings we hunger for recurring experience. This helps to explain both the cyclical nature of mythology and a fundamental element of story: The details mentioned early in the story usually recur, often with more significance, toward the end of the story. No accident that Cinderella lost a slipper while running from the ball. No coincidence that Piggy's glasses are used to start a fire early in *Lord of the Flies.* These details help set up the events that will follow. And, sure enough, they reappear later in the story.

"If in the first chapter you say that a gun hung on the wall," Chekhov said, "in the second or third chapter it must without fail be discharged."

In Aliki's picture book *The Two of Them,* the grandfather makes a ring for his granddaughter on the day of her birth. The girl grows up, spending long stretches of time with her grandfather. The ring makes a few sly appearances in the book's lovely illustrations but does not get mentioned in the text until a crucial moment in the book:

> Time passed,
> and the ring fit the little girl's finger,
> and it seemed, suddenly,

that grandfather was an old man.
One night he became ill,
and after that,
part of him could not move.

In Aliki's book, the ring would seem to work on many levels: keepsake, sign of the girl's maturity, symbol suggesting the circularity of life.

Many young writers have a difficult time juggling the details in their writing. Frank, a second grader, wrote:

> A boy went into the forest. He found a frog and put it into his pocket. He kept walking and found an old house. An old man lived there. He invited the boy into the house for lunch. "Okay," said the boy.

The story continued for many pages. It turned out that the old man was a dangerous wizard out to capture the little boy for his wicked purposes. I had a writing conference with Frank.

"What I'm wondering is, what happened to the frog?" I asked. "I kept expecting to hear about that frog in the boy's pocket."

Frank looked surprised.

"Oh, there's not going to be anything else about the frog," he explained, shrugging. "That was just the beginning of the story." He was utterly unaware of the expectation he had raised in his reader.

A detail mentioned early that shows up later can provide a deeply satisfying resolution to any piece of writing. Genevieve, a fourth grader, wrote this story:

THE SAD DAYS

> When I was four years old I used to have a blanket I would carry around. But one Sunday morning I woke up and it wasn't there. I asked my mom where Mr. Blanky was and she said: "It's in the attic." I said: "Why is it in the attic?" and she said: "You are growing up now. You're not supposed to carry a blanket around." So I went to my room and cried.
>
> On my birthday when I turned five years old my mommy gave me a teddy bear. I was so happy then I started holding that all the time. But one day my father was so mad he stole it away

from me because every time I started walking with it I would knock things down. He put it in the attic with Mr. Blanky.

One rainy afternoon my mom started screaming and I was scared but then my father called Grandma to stay with us while Mommy and Daddy went to the hospital. A couple of days later she came back crying and I asked her why she was crying and she said: "I lost the baby." I said: "What?" She said she had a miscarriage but I didn't understand.

When I was seven years old I asked her again and she explained it to me. Then I went upstairs in the attic, took down Mr. Blanky, and gave it to my mom to make her feel better because Mr. Blanky always made me feel better every time I was sad.

The recurring detail works like an echo in which the second mention is nearly always more important than the first. In the following poem of mine, a jug of cider gets hidden in a river at the beginning of the poem. The jug of cider recurs at the end of the poem, hopefully transformed into something larger than itself.

River Heart

Close to the moist bank of the creek
my brother and I enter the forest.
We hide a jug of fresh apple cider,
wedged underwater between mossy stones,
and follow the stream up forest.

Later it gets hot and we branch off
through a stand of stunted pines
with bear tracks and deer droppings.
Everything here is dark and still.
We sit down to share our only apple.
"We're lost," my little brother sighs
and tries mightily not to cry.
The trees have veins like Mom's legs,
hiding us under huge hushed skirts.
Tons of raw pine creak above us.

The wind dies and Bobby jumps up:
"I hear the river calling to us!"

Off he goes and finds the creek!
It curves and hisses and glistens,
a silver snake caressed by the sun.
We race downstream to the wet place
where the cider alone awaits our return.
I lift it out, dripping, triumphant,
an icy throbbing river heart.

We drink it slowly
walking home
and I feel the river's pulse
in my bones.

Five

CREATING A CHARACTER

*A writer should know how much change
a character has in his pockets.*

—JAMES JOYCE

I CONDUCTED an intense poetry seminar with two dozen teachers and administrators in Burlington, Massachusetts. We spent an hour writing poems of our own. Just before lunch I asked if anyone would like to read aloud what they had written. Awkward pause. Carla Panciera, a teacher I had just met that day, tentatively raised her hand.

"It's not quite done," she said, "but I'll read it."

One Piece of My Father

*A "v" revealed through the neck
of his cotton shin, a triangle
two fingers spread could frame,
perfect, brown as his face,
the disturbed earth, my eyes
that are, instead, my mother's.
The corner of him that knows
the sun up close
from high on a tractor
pacing the horizon, or
from a barn he shingles
with the cedar he cut months ago
when the swamp was frozen,
or looking up the way he did*

to judge a piece of sky:
sun for hay, rain for corn,
clouds for relief, a small space
of man, a glimpse of work,
a spot to rest against, up close
to ask a question to
to force him to look down.

When she finished reading there was a long pause. Sensing that no one else would dare follow that poem, I said: "Well, I guess it's time for lunch."

A story requires the intersection of three spheres:

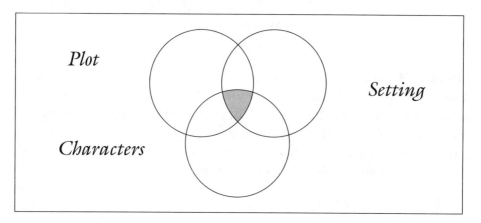

Innumerable links, large and small, connect these three elements. Character drives plot (Ahab is obsessed with killing the white whale), which gets sculpted by the setting (the man makes one last attempt to build a fire, but it is seventy-five degrees below zero and his hands have grown numb), which, in turn, is affected by the characters in the story (the soldiers set fire to the plantation).

But character remains preeminent. The characters contain the crucial human link, that element of human destiny, for the reader to identify with.

Writers will forever wrestle with the challenge of creating characters that get up off the page and step into our lives. Great writers use a few deft strokes or odd details to create characters with an apparent effortlessness that takes our breath away. Suddenly, we feel we have known them our entire lives: Buck or Charlotte, Randall McMurphy or Scarlett O'Hara.

When I set out to create a character, either a real or imagined person, I try for a healthy balance between their public and private persona:

PUBLIC
Accomplishments
Biographical background
Appearance

PRIVATE
Emotions
Quirks
Inner strengths and fears

Whether trying to describe a historical figure (presidents, baseball players, explorers, inventors) or a fictional character (human being or animal), young writers need help in breathing life into their characters. These writers typically find it easier to describe a character's public persona than to reveal what readers really want: a sense of the character's inner being, i.e., what makes him or her tick.

THE PHYSICAL BEING

"After World War II, I used to go to a lot of dances," Bill Gregory, a retired teacher, told me. "I could always tell which of the young women had been working in a factory during the war. It wasn't just their skin, which was too white. It wasn't just that pinched look around their eyes. It was their hands. The factory girls were the ones who always had calluses on their palms."

Our bodies are maps that tell the stories of our lives: triumphs, scars, stamina, the inroads of death. When writers explore the terrain of the physical, we help readers enter more fully into the life of our characters. Here is a fine opportunity for writers to use their most important tools—the five senses.

Touch: "When Grandpa kissed me goodnight his stubbly cheek felt like a piece of old sandpaper from the garage."

Taste: "Grandma sliced cantaloupe on the same old cutting board she had used to cut innumerable cloves of garlic, so a bite of melon set off a war in my mouth between juicy sweetness and garlicky tang."

Sound: "In the morning, I listened to my mother trying to clear her lungs. Some days she'd hack away for a half hour or forty minutes. She had two distinct kinds of coughs. The wet one sounded like each lung was snarled in long wet strips of cloth. The dry cough sounded like the last few nails being pounded into a block of wood, or a coffin. . . ."

Sight: "She had long arms and bony elbows. When she cut her meat, she reminded me of one of those big sea birds awkwardly flapping its wings, trying to gain altitude."

Smell: "She worked in a candy store, and the smell of fudge permeated her clothing; my mouth watered whenever she gave me a hug."

When students write about someone familiar, such as a mother or close friend, they often have a too deeply internalized sense of the person or pet to describe the character with real objectivity. Such writers may not realize that the words on the page do not provide enough information for the reader to form a clear image of the character. In such cases, a writing teacher might invite the student to literally "flesh out" the character by using the five senses.

I talked with Meredith, a second grader who had just written the first draft of the following poem:

Grand Parents

My grandpa is still alive . . .
My grandma is dead ohh poo!
Oh, why did you die?

"It's not very good," Meredith said. "It's so short."

"Is the poem about your grandmother or your grandfather?" I asked her.

"My grandmother, really."

"Your grandmother. Well, here's a suggestion. How about if you just concentrate on her?"

"All right."

"Help me picture her."

"Well, she had a really big warm smile," Meredith said. "She had curly gold hair. . . ."

A few minutes later, Meredith had tried a slightly more expansive draft of her poem:

she is beautiful
she has a warm smile
she has brown eyes
she also has curly hair
that's my grandma

When Meredith and I talked some more, I encouraged her to teach me everything she knew about her grandmother. Her final draft showed little resemblance to what she started with.

<u>Special Ending</u>

She's beautiful
Warm smile
Brown eyes
Curly gold hair

Lived near me
Went to parks
Sailed boats

Now she's dead
Left behind for me
Golden earrings
They mean the world to me.

THE TELLING DETAIL

Deft characterization can be slow, painstaking work, though it doesn't have to be laborious. Sometimes a writer can bring a character to life with a single, carefully chosen detail. There is an art to this, of course; find the right specific and every aspect of the character comes into instant focus for the reader, right down to the color of his socks, her earrings.

I know a woman, a phenomenal cook. Cream of carrot soup that would make you weep. If you ask for the recipe, she'll give it to you, carefully typed, with an obliging smile. Unfortunately, she has already subtly altered the ingredients. No matter how hard you try, no matter how painstakingly you follow her recipe, your soup will never approach hers.

His mother fed him four slices of white bread before dinner so he wouldn't eat too much meat.

The boy rode on his brand new bicycle, down the driveway, onto the sidewalk and—crash! He fell forward, right onto his face. He lay there motionless. The bike continued a few feet further before it, too, slammed into the pavement, the front wheel still spinning. With a cry his mother rushed down the driveway, past her son, and bent to examine the bicycle.

In a gangster novel, the author introduced a dangerous young man: "He was a well-dressed young man, and he wore cufflinks reputedly made from human bone."

In *Miss Maggie,* a picture book by Cynthia Rylant, Nat, a boy, develops a friendship with Miss Maggie, an elderly Appalachian woman. Here's an excerpt:

Sometimes Miss Maggie rode to the grocery store with Nat and his grandfather. Nat would wait in the truck when Miss Maggie went into the store, because she always had a wad of tobacco in her jaw and she'd spit it just anywhere she pleased. Nat was afraid people might think she was a relative.

That single detail—spitting tobacco juice inside a store—goes a long way toward convincing the reader that this woman is an outsider who has never wholly adapted herself to mainstream society.

The revelatory detail can also act as a dramatic clue to show a character undergoing a crucial metamorphosis. For example, my grandfather was a fastidious dresser. Even on a summer day of eighty degrees, he would come downstairs wearing a clean white shirt, tie, light jacket, with every hair in place. One time when my grandfather came to visit I noticed that he was as impeccably dressed as usual except for one thing: his belt was outside one of the loops in his pants. I didn't say anything, but two mornings later I noticed Grandpa's belt had missed two loops on one side, and one loop on the other.

The bigger the issue, the smaller you write. Don't write about senility or a man losing the ability to take care of himself. Write about missed belt loops. Put forth the raw evidence, and trust that the reader will understand exactly what you are getting at.

SPOKEN WORDS

Peter is a smoker, in his fifties somewhere, with deep lines on his face. A face showing character and suffering. When I met Peter, my first reaction was that his face had melted and slipped about two inches. He had a Catholic school background. My overall impression was that he should have retired a long time ago. The man is nasty to his ninth-grade students, even with me sitting there in the classroom.

"Look at that," he barks at one student. "Hey, what, can you read that? Do you include a magnifying glass with your story? Write larger!"

His students are silent as he moves around the room.

"Michael, I'm confused about something. Are *you* the teacher? Oh, I see. *I* am. So hey, when I say you need to change your conclusion, I mean *change* it. *Improve* it."

At one point Peter loudly crumples up one girl's story and throws it into the gray wastepaper basket. Still glaring at the girl, he rushes to the front of the room and grabs a piece of chalk.

"A map!" he shouts. "M–A–P. The assignment was to map out your story *before* you write. What, hey, am I speaking Swahili here or what?"

Peter quickly sketches a map of New York with Long Island, a horizontal fish, at the bottom.

"Here's Nassau County," he says, marking it with an X. "Here's Albany. How do I get there?"

One boy cautiously raises his hand; Peter jabs a finger at him.

"Drive?"

"All right, you can drive!" Peter roars back. "Fine! Is there just one way of getting there?"

"No?"

"No!" He's on a roll now; he speaks in rapid rhythm. "You can take the Taconic State Parkway. You can take the New York State Thruway. You can go over to Jersey and take Route 17 north. There's all kinds of ways to go. How do you know which one to use?"

"Look at a map?" one boy timidly suggests.

"Right!" Peter is nearly beside himself. "You look at a map to plan your route! What do—look, I don't care which way you go, but I want to know that *you* know which way you're going. Make a map first! That's what I've been trying to tell you! My point is—and follow the map when you write! And if you start writing something that's *not* on the map—what? What?"

Pause. The students stare at him.

Peter screams: "You're *on the wrong road!*"

We reveal ourselves by what we say, how we say it, what we do not say. A writer develops an ear for dialogue by learning how to eavesdrop: listening to the spoken word.

John Burningham's timeless picture book *Granpa* contains a series of moments between a girl and her grandfather. The book is written almost entirely in simple dialogue, without speaker tags, so the reader is invited to figure out just who says what. My favorite page reads:

> "When we get to the beach can we stay there forever?"
> "Yes, but we must come home for our tea at four o'clock."

Even the youngest reader can see that the word "forever" is a potent clue that the words of the first sentence were spoken by the child.

Written dialogue, when it sounds authentic, is filled with the grammatical errors, sentence fragments, interruptions, grunts, sighs, and spontaneous wit that make human speech what it is. It is important to learn to listen—not to what a person is trying to say but what that person actually says.

Andrew is an extraordinarily gifted second grader from Mount Prospect, Illinois. One morning he had a peer conference with a girl in the class.

"What are you writing about today?" he asks.

"I think I'm going to write about my dog who died."

"That's the spirit!" Andrew says cheerfully. The boy laughs and glances at the teacher. "Get it, Mrs. Weiss? The dog died! *That's the spirit!*"

Later that day, Janet Weiss puts the kids through a basic math review. Andrew groans.

"Aw Mrs. Weiss, if I'd known that this was all I was going to learn today I would've stayed on the bus."

Spoken dialogue has the uncanny ability to conjure up an entire world. I collect in my journal stray bits of dialogue, snatches of conversation that evoke a mood or a bigger, though unspoken, issue. One morning, while walking in the park, I came upon a couple, around thirty, arguing on a bench.

"I'm tired of riding the rollercoaster of your moods," the woman hissed in a whisper. "I want to get off!"

I stole this snippet of dialogue and jotted it in my notebook for possible future use.

In a first-grade classroom, a girl has just read her cat story to the class. When she finishes a boy raises his hand.

"You need to keep your cat in a cage," he says.

"No, we don't do that," the girl replies.

"Well, the cat'll scratch up the furniture."

"We don't have a cage. My mother puts patches on the furniture."

"Wow," the boy says. "Your mom is nice!"

"She is nice." The girl pauses. "To cats."

"If I was a cat," the boy says, "I'd go live with your mom."

GESTURE AND MOTION

Taylor is never so content as when he's sitting next to his mother, the two fingers of his right hand stuck in his mouth, the fingers of the other hand playing with JoAnn's exuberant hair. He plays with it idly, glancing up now and then at the dark mass, then down, twirling it tight, letting it come loose, a motion that reminds me of nothing so much as the cotton candy makers at the fair, wrapping sugary webs around the thin white paper cones.

At 6:30 A.M. Adam makes his first down payment on breakfast: a big bowl of Golden Graham cereal with milk. He gulps it down quickly. In between bites, he races from the table to his spot in front of the television, a ring of milk around his mouth, then back again when his mouth is empty. Later, when JoAnn and I have breakfast, Adam is there for his second installment, whatever we are having: pancakes, oatmeal, scrambled eggs, or a blueberry muffin. He is fully capable of three such breakfasts before he finally quits eating, secure in the knowledge that lunch is not too far off.

The kids who are best at playing war are the kids who know how to die the best. Every kid knows this. This was true when I was young, and I would be surprised if it were not equally true today. When I played war nobody could die more fiercely, more convincingly, than my old friend Freddy Fletcher (no relation). His deaths had a life of their own: the sudden slack-jawed clutch at his wounded torso, the long, drawn-out virulent howl, the sound of a final breath being ripped from his lungs. His frame had a strange way of hanging there, twisting, for a few seconds. Then his body went board-rigid, already a victim of rigor mortis, a moment before he hurtled forward and down onto the hard ground. "He's dead, all right," I'd mutter to myself, even as I marveled at how he had managed to avoid mashing his nose on the ground.

Get your characters moving. There's an old saying that you can tell more about a man by the way he cuts his meat than by anything he says. Two boys go into the forest for a picnic. One boy has brought some juice, potato chips, and two apples. The other boy has brought a whole small cooked chicken.

When they begin eating, the first boy rips off an entire chicken leg and begins gnawing hungrily. The other boy wrinkles his nose, takes out a gleaming knife, cuts off a single slice of white meat from the very top of the chicken, and places it carefully on a napkin. He takes out a fork and begins to eat.

Gestures can clearly reveal a character's emotional or physical state, as in this tender poem by Michelle, a second grader:

Only with Him

Only with him
I love to stay.
He is very busy
but he could find
some time to stay
with me.
I love going to the
movies with him
where it's dark.
Even though he
falls asleep.
I still love my father.

THE "FLASH-DRAFT" AS A TOOL FOR NONFICTION WRITING

Soft feet pound the ground. A sleek, shiny body pounces on a young deer. Strong claws break the deer's neck. The cougar, Ghost of the Rockies, has made its kill.

Strictly carnivorous, the cougar's chief prey are deer and elk. . . .

JoAnn Portalupi first conceived of the "flash-draft" as a way to help students internalize information and to write more lively nonfiction. The student begins by creating a specific character and by putting that character into a brief scene, anecdote, or story. The flash-draft might never become part of the final piece. But by having the student focus on one specific character at one particular moment, the flash-draft gives students a narrative vehicle for bringing alive that character and the larger world in which that character lives.

One group of third graders wrote flash-drafts for the animals they were studying.

> One morning when the panda woke up, his zookeeper was right outside his cage with an apple for breakfast. On the other side of the world the panda's brother is laying down on the grass chewing the bamboo leaves.
> *Scott S.*

Lindsey brought her animal alive using a comparison between the animal's life and her own:

> When I'm getting ready for bed the panther wakes up from its sleep and goes hunting for its prey. Then, so no animal can touch the panther's food, it goes up to the top of the tree carrying its prey and comes back with more food for her cubs.

I was sufficiently impressed by the voice and energy in these third graders' writing that I decided to road test the flash-draft idea with a group of fifth-grade students that had been studying South American cultures.

"Put your notes away," I said to the students. "I want you to think of a character and see if you can put that character into a story. You might pick a famous character or an ordinary person. Make it as true, as authentic, as you possibly can. You might try to use what you've learned about weather or geography in your flash-draft."

Jessica Abrams wrote about a poor mountain girl:

> Waneta woke up at five o'clock in the morning. As she walks outside, she sees how high up she is. Waneta lives in Lima, Peru. She is poor. Her family grows food such as cabbages. It is very hard to grow food in the poor soil of the Andes mountains. Waneta is ten years old. She sits down and braids her hair with one, long, shiny black braid. It is a tradition in her town for everybody to wear a braid. . . .

Jessica's flash-draft has much to commend it: a sense of place, an attention to the particular. But for me, at least, it works primarily because I believe in the character of Waneta, who springs to life in my imagination through that "one, long, shiny black braid."

I suggested the flash-draft to an eighth-grade English class that had been studying topics related to the Great Depression. The flash-drafts were written during class time and entirely without notes; the best of them showed a skillful interweaving of information and narrative, anchored by a single character at the center.

WALT DISNEY

Amy gripped the armrest of the chair with her hands. Her palms were sweaty with excitement. Finally, her mother had taken her to see the new film: "Snow White and the Seven Dwarfs." Amy remembered when Walt Disney had first created Mickey Mouse. Now he was her hero. The lights dimmed: the show was about to begin.

Walt Disney, a hero of children of all ages, was called the "master of make-believe." He, like many others, was brought down by the Depression in the early 30s. Disney made many cartoons including "The Three Little Pigs." The song "Who's Afraid of the Big Bad Wolf" referred to the big bad social wolf . . . the Depression. Disney's song became very popular, and was played almost as often as the other songs of the ages.

In 1935 Walt Disney won a medal for Mickey Mouse calling him a "symbol of international good will." Disney's cheery characters helped many people through tough times.

As Amy left the movie theatre she felt very happy. Things were hard at home, but she felt good knowing that at the movies there would always be a happy ending.

VOICE

Writing with voice is writing into which someone has breathed. It has that fluency, rhythm, and liveliness that exist naturally in the speech of most people when they are enjoying a conversation. . . . Writing with real voice has the power to make you pay attention and understand—the words go deep.

—PETER ELBOW, *Writing with Power*

THE FOLLOWING PIECE was written by an eighth-grade boy:

THE COMPOSITION

Boy, this burns me up. I look around the room, and everyone is writing except for me. There is only one thing flashing through my mind. "What should I write about?" I always feel there is a black hole inside of me regarding a topic.

I always get hot under the collar when my English teacher asks what we are up to in our compositions. Everyone says, "Second draft" or "Finished." I usually say: "First draft" and everyone around me gives me the evil eye. I try to remember experiences in my life that I could write about but nothing comes to mind. And even if I get an idea on paper, it never works out the way I want.

Every teacher says don't worry about the grammar, punctuation, and spelling until you edit your work: just get something down on your paper. I worry about the grammar even before I write a piece, which confuses me. With every piece I write, there is always something telling me that people are not going to like it. This ruins my train of thought.

Then there is a problem I have expressing my thoughts. I can tell someone a story but can't describe it on a piece of paper. When I write a piece I am proud of, it usually receives a bad grade, but when write a piece I don't like, it usually receives a fairly good grade.

One of the two things that distresses me most is when I see people whose pieces are two or three pages long. Then I look at my composition, and it is only one page long. This makes me believe that the people with bigger compositions are going to get a better grade because their composition is longer than mine. Some kids in class come up to me and ask if the teacher accepts my one page composition.

"Yes, he does." For this reason alone I am going to end this piece here.

The last chapter explored ways of creating character. But one character that writers most consistently fail to develop is the narrator. Too often the narrator (or main character) becomes little more than observer, a neutral teller-of-tales about whose inner life we learn little. Writing of this kind lacks *voice*.

People get confused about voice. What is it? Style? Tone? Is it always informal?

When I talk about voice, I mean written words that carry with them the sense that someone has actually written them. Not a committee, not a computer: a single human being. Writing with voice has the same quirky cadence that makes human speech so impossible to resist listening to. Dark humor, numerous cryptic asides, and a terrific ending make "The Composition" such a pleasure to read. The author creates an ironic tension between his topic (an inability to write well) and the composition itself, which is written with real authority. This writing has energy: juice.

Many people who are charming in person find it difficult to sound natural, to sound like themselves on the page. Developing voice in one's writing requires awareness and diligence; it probably also requires a patient, supportive mentor or writing teacher. Those of us who work with young writers might consider a two-stage approach for encouraging students to develop voice: helping them explore their "inner writing voice," and showing them ways of keeping some of that voice intact when the writing goes public, goes formal.

STALKING YOUR INNER VOICE

While working on this book, I realized that writing really does have a kind of symmetry. A balancing act. Tension and resolution. Dramatic scene and narrative summary. Action and reflection. A beginning that fits with the ending.

Likewise, the writer balances the characters' external and internal lives. And one way of revealing the internal life of the narrator or other character is through the inner voice.

Everyone has an inner voice. But the writer is different from everyone else; the writer listens. She pays attention to the inner voice. Frequently she will drop everything to write down whatever it has to say. If the inner voice gets skittish at her approach, she tries sneaking up to it. Coos soothingly. Tries tossing out a few crumbs. The writer may not know exactly what the inner voice represents (unconscious? superego? spirit?) but the writer does know one thing: the inner voice is spokesperson for the inner life.

In Annie Dillard's *Pilgrim at Tinker Creek,* there is a marvelous essay on stalking the misunderstood muskrat. Toward the end the author asserts: "You have to stalk the spirit, too."

The writer must learn how to stalk the inner voice; at least I find I must. It whispers to me continuously, all year, but the pace of my life makes it difficult to tune in. To tune inward. And when I finally get around to doing so, all too often the inner voice bolts. Vanishes.

I stalk my inner voice in my writer's notebook. These blank pages provide a safe space where I can write comfortably, chatting on paper, chumming up to my—what? Consciousness? Mind's eye? I don't really know what to call it, though it is probably the central tool I have as a writer.

In this notebook I try to slow down. Give each thought its due, its space. For example: I have discovered that I like writing on the right side of my journal better than the left. The pages lie flatter.

Up early, play with Robert while JoAnn sleeps, then bring him upstairs for a second round of nursing. Back downstairs, I immediately set to stalking (I once wrote *wiretapping*) my inner voice. 7:30 A.M. Eerie quiet outside. The deck is moist with dew. I can hear a trickle from the brook. I walk with bare feet over wet grass to the far edge of the lawn. Looking back at the house, I see a large skunk sauntering across the wooden bridge of the creek. Sauntering like he owns the place. Which I suppose he does.

Thoreau once wrote an essay where he talked about the word *saunter.* He was talking about walking, a leisurely kind of walking and reflecting on life. *Saunter*, Thoreau suggested, might have been derived from the French words *sans* and *terre* ("without the earth"). When you saunter, you are not rooted to the physical earth. Rather, you can let your thoughts wander.

That seems like the perfect word for a writer's notebook. Time enough (and room enough) to saunter.

I come back to the house, make coffee, bring it outside to the table I'm writing on. I read a magazine. The tall flower—larkspur?—growing at the edge of the deck is the most vivid purple I have ever seen. The purple challenges me: C'mon, write something good.

I'm stalking, all right, but I can tell it will be a slow approach. Having trouble locking in the proper frequency. Dillard names the old classic rule about stalking: "Stop often 'n set frequent." I am stopping. I am setting. Trying to be patient.

First, this stray bit of consciousness to attend to—strange, true, nearly forgotten in the grinding rush to finish up work. For the past ten days or so I have stumbled out of bed in the morning with the name Cory McFlintock in my mind. She—only her name (*Is* Cory always a girl's name?)—appears most distinctly when I stagger into the bathroom, take off my pj's, and start my shower.

I have no explanation for this. Maybe I heard the name somewhere (the radio?) and it got buried in my memory. Still, why should it persist for two weeks in coloring the beginnings of each day? Who are you Cory McFlintock, and what do you want from me?

Tomorrow I will take this chair and place it on the wooden bridge. Let the tumbling waters below whisper encouragement to my inner voice: flow, words. Flow, memory.

It's painful getting back in touch with my inner voice. It forces me to ask big grown-up questions about my life. When you have been tied up for several hours, the first sensation you get upon being untied is one of excruciating pain as the blood flows back and remembers (!) the areas that have been cut off from circulation. Bring a frostbitten person into a warm house, he or she will be fine until the frozen extremities start thawing out. Then cover your ears.

My inner voice, long ignored, finally attended to, responds by howling bitterly. Where the hell have *you* been? Do you think you can snap me on and off like a radio? Take a good look at yourself. You are a writer, a poet. When you ignore me, you ignore yourself.

I have no suitable response save to write it all down. Just possibly Cynthia Rylant and Jane Yolen were right when they suggested, in separate interviews with me, the notion of some higher power that writes *through* them. Why not? I'm willing to believe in the magic. I'm going to put a piece of apple pie and a carrot right by the fireplace, right beneath the hung stockings. When static obscures the inner voice, when the tracks get faint, I will read, breathe, talk a walk, dream, play with my son. Wait and see what happens.

Wait. Franz Kafka had the motto—*Warte*—written on the wall above his bed. Sounds easy, but who has the time or the patience for waiting?

(Later, the inner voice started flowing, not when I expected, while I was ready, notebook open, pen in hand, but while I was playing with Robert and studying his two-month-old head. It didn't flow in complete sentences either, but in fragments. Words.)

Newspapers trumpeting global warming. Global thawing between the U.S. and the Soviets. Emerging global economy. The globe of Robert's little head. JoAnn: "Don't you just love the changing topography of his face?" The top of his head resembles the Arctic Circle: tundra, not much growing up there. Wide expanses of skull, scalp, thinly growing hair. The soft spot: fontanel. Etymology of that word? Check. Expandable skull for a mushrooming brain. Seen from above, the fontanel looks exactly like adult-sized lips. Like something dark has bent down to put its kiss, the imprint of its lips, on Robert's head. Makes me hold him more tightly.

His hair: fine, brown, a hint of red under certain light. JoAnn's father laughed, never seen an Italian baby with reddish hair. Thin as my own hair.

Eyebrows (barely visible) forming a line along the globe's equator. Major facial features (eyes, ears, nose, mouth) all scrunched down below this equator.

His eyes are surprisingly, exuberantly blue. Temporary? They will fade to brown, we think, though we are prepared to be surprised. Eyes alert, expressive, cross-eyed at times. Heavy and swollen after he nurses. Eyeballs soaked in milk.

(Sometimes the inner voice doesn't whisper—it screams.)

Robert is six months old. At the supermarket people stare and lavish attention on Robert. "What a little doll," one lady says. To her seven-year-old: "Wouldn't you love to find *that* under the Christmas tree on Christmas morning?"

I smile tensely, make my exit, but my inner voice is berserk: "Look, lady, he's *not* some little doll. He's a complex little human, a Homo sapiens seething with instinct, emotion, song, story, archetype, and language. Get back! Don't you dare put a bow on my son!"

Then again, it's possible that fatherhood has made me somewhat high-strung.

One use of the notebook is to jump-start the mind. But another purpose, equally important, is to provide a place to relax, to settle into a comfortable writing stride. I try to let some of that easy notebookish voice leak into the writing I do for publication. It is an indirect process. I think of my readers as one person. I figure that if that person can get a sense of me as a person he might, in turn, listen to what I have to say.

Helping young writers find this inner voice starts with time—giving young writers the regular time they need. A five-minute "journal write" first thing each morning, while the teacher takes lunch count, probably isn't enough. They need sustained time.

"Too often in classrooms we give children little squirts of language," Bill Martin Jr. once said to me. "We squirt at them, and they squirt back."

We can also teach students to revise for voice. Read it back. Listen to how the writing sounds. Which parts sound most like you? Are there places where you can hear yourself chatting to a friend? Do certain parts sound stiff and awkwardly formal? Listen for real voice in these two sentences: "We rode rapidly to the store" or "We raced to the store."

Voice is connected to real audience. We must create classrooms where students have a wide, sympathetic audience for their writing. We need to encourage students to meet their audience in authentic ways—not just during share sessions with their peers but also by going public with their writing in other ways beyond the walls of the classroom: complaint letters, articles, contests, etc.

FINDING A WRITING VOICE

The poet Suzanne Gardinier says that voice in writing has much to do with an *intimacy* between writer and subject: a closeness between the author and what is being written about. In voiceless writing, the author stands far back from the subject. Such distance can impart a cold, detached feel to the writing. When writing has real voice, you can sense the author pulling in close, cozying up to the subject, as in the poem by Danielle, a first-grade writer (see Figure 6-1).

I love the boldness of that first line—ho I sey—the utter lack of artifice. I can just picture this first grader beaming as she announces her wonder to the world.

It's not uncommon to find young children writing with voice. For older students, however, writing with real voice becomes more the exception than the rule. I have worked in many upper-grade classrooms populated by young writers who have lost their voice.

Figure 6-1

Danielle 1/28/

hO I sey.

Culrd pant.

in the sgi.

it macks a

reabow.

What kills it? I'd finger *audience* as the major murder suspect. As students get older, the audience for their writing undergoes a shift. As they approach adolescence, they tend to become more self-critical, particularly in terms of writing. This internal shift gets reinforced by tougher demands from the outside world. The supportive writing environment in the primary grades, often flavored with a child-centered or developmental philosophy about learning, yields to upper-grade realities of grading, book reports, grammar worksheets, and five-paragraph essays. The stifling focus on AYP and state writing tests certainly doesn't help, either.

Voice is one area where older writers can learn from younger ones. Often, the work of young writers contains an intimacy not just between the writer and subject but also between writer and audience. Young writers regularly demonstrate an uncanny ability to reach out from the page, to converse freely with the reader. Lauren, a second-grade girl, wrote:

> Hi these are my frends. see my perins are divores. it isn't fun having perins ho ar divres't ao I omost frgot My name is Lauren. at frest youl do a lot of crying. but you'l get uest to it. you now it didin't tarn awt so bad see. but after a long time don't think you are the one ho made the divores beeas It wasin't it was bitwene your perens so i tink divors is fun in a way so see evn thowe your perins are divors it still is fun living withaut your Mom are dad by the way tangnks for lisining!
>
> Hi. These are my friends. See, my parents are divorced. It isn't fun having parents who are divorced. Oh, I almost forgot, my name is Lauren. At first you'll do a lot of crying. But you'll get used to it. You know, it didn't turn out so bad, see? But after a long time don't think you are the one who made the divorce because it wasn't, it was between your parents. So I think divorce is fun in a way. So even though your parents are divorced it still is fun living without your Mom or Dad. By the way, thanks for listening!

It is rarer to see a story with voice from an older student. This story was written by Gina Pedone, a twelve-year-old writer from Merrick, New York. The searching honesty coupled with the narrator's self-knowledge makes the voice sound so authentic.

> When my brother was born, he wasn't exactly a bouncing baby boy. He had a lot of problems with his insides, and well I just couldn't understand it then. I was still waiting for my teeth to come out for the tooth fairy.
>
> A lot of times mom would stay at the hospital helping the nurse care for the sick child. Back then I didn't know what was happening and I got jealous. He got cared for 24 hours a day

and I got stuck with next-door neighbors who tried feeding me orange marmalade sandwiches.

After five operations the doctors said he was well enough to come home. Just to look at him would bring tears to your eyes. He was always pale and had to be fed through a tube from inside his stomach. A lot of times he would pull out the tube and we would have to rush him to the hospital so it could be put back in. It was horrible.

After a few more operations the tube went away and he was beginning to look normal. Today he still goes for check-ups and he has epilepsy but mostly he is a regular, annoying, bratty younger sibling. Thank God he is!

The following story, by Luke, a fifth grader, uses interior monologue to create a voice of convincing authority. By the end of this story, I had come to believe in this mirror's ability to talk to me.

How come, out of all the mirrors in the world, they had to pick me to be in a Penn Station bathroom? Why? I absolutely hate it.

The reason why I hate it so much is because of the gangs and businessmen who come in here. The businessmen come in like a bunch of wild cattle. They come in with no respect at all! None! As they come in here, they laugh like this: "Hardy har har har!" Supposedly they were laughing about some corny joke. They think they are so cool with their cashmere suits and their silk ties. But they are not cool, they are corny!

Lots of gangs come in here with their black leather jackets and weird haircuts. They smell like skunks with their so-called cologne. Sometimes with their switchblades they carve letters into me like M.C. likes J.P. You probably think that doesn't hurt me because I am a mirror, but it really does hurt. It's like getting a deep cut on your stomach and then squeezing lemon juice on it. It kills.

If I could talk to all these people I would say: "Please don't mess me up anymore because I am already badly messed up. I wouldn't like to die a miserable mirror with carvings all over me. I would like to die happy."

One day I was minding my own business when two en-emies from different gangs came into the bathroom. They started quarrelling. Then they started fist fighting. One guy started jumping around like a frog and another one started punching like a professional boxer. Suddenly the guy who was jumping got the other guy from the shoulders and threw him at me. I cracked and shattered. The gang member who got thrown into me had a bloody nose.

Well here I am. All broken. Hey! What's this man doing in here? Hey, get off me now! Don't take me off this wall! I admit it: I love it here! It's home to me! No, don't throw me in the garbage! No! Oh! No! I guess I am going to die! I am not going to cry. I sure hope I will go to the big bathroom in the sky. Here comes the dump truck. Goodbye world! Goodbye!

VOICE IN NONFICTION WRITING

A friend of mine once found herself in the middle of a divorce. In January her soon-to-be-ex-husband asked if he might use the house one last time to throw a party. She consented, with one caveat: She requested that he and his guests take particular care with her plants. The house was filled with many species of tropical plants from around the world. He nodded wearily; he knew all about the plants. Not to worry, he told her.

She went away the weekend of his party. An hour before the party, he brought all the plants outside, in sub-zero temperature. After the party, he brought them all inside again. The plants didn't look too bad when she returned home. But within a week every one of them had died.

This nasty (I first wrote "chilling" but decided the pun might be distracting and work against the impact of the story) tale comes to mind when I think of the transition we ask student writers to make from expressive (narrative and poetry) to nonfiction writing. In trying to make this shift, many teachers have found the old cliché proven true: The operation is a success but the patient dies. The kids grudgingly make the transition, but the voice in their writing doesn't survive.

The switch from narrative to information writing does not seem nearly so traumatic for primary children. Often the nonfiction writing of young children shows a comfortable mix of information with their own zest and passion, as in this report by a first grader:

All abowt thee oyl spil	*All About the Oil Spill*
by Lauren Loewy	by Lauren Loewy

Some of thee ana	Some of the
moise did from thee	animals died from the
oyl spil	oil spill.
The worter	The water
wosint Blue	wasn't blue
It Was Black	it was black.
I wish Exxon	I wish Exxon
wad cleth up the Werter.	would clean up the water.
I reyly fyl	I really feel
Mad.	mad.
and ain gry	and angry
ryly ain gry	. . . really angry!!!

Upper-grade writers have more trouble imbuing their nonfiction writing with voice, especially when research is involved. Mary K. Healy has noted that the nonfiction of older students is often characterized by "dump-truck writing": students who pick up a clump of words (usually copied from a website), drop those words onto the paper, and are genuinely surprised when teachers accuse them of plagiarism.

Reading is a critical step in fostering voice in nonfiction writing. Students need to spend lots of time reading information books that are written with voice—*Can We Save The Tiger?* by Martin Jenkins, *I Stink!* by Kate McMullan, and *Bugs* by Nancy Winslow Parker and Joan Richards Wright. We might invite students to compare the voice in these nonfiction books to encyclopedia texts on the same subjects. Our students cannot write in a vacuum: They need to get an image, a vision, of what their writing might look like in this genre.

As they start a unit on nonfiction writing, I suggest that teachers spend an hour a day for at least a week reading and rereading selected books in this genre with their class. Students should concentrate not just on *what* the authors are saying but, more importantly, *how* they are saying it. Teachers might take time to help students study the various techniques being used: humor, rhyme, myth/truth, question/answer, diagrams, interview, fantasy. All these techniques are available for students to use in their own nonfiction writing.

Voice in writing has to do with a unique personality-on-paper. But some writers find their voice by imitating other writers. Andrew Merton, who teaches writing at the University of New Hampshire, suggests that students find a journalist whose style appeals to them and imitate that writer's voice. By imitating another writer, you sometimes give yourself the freedom to find your own voice. I know I went through my own "Hemingway period"—trying to write those lean, muscular sentences. Later, I fell in love with the irreverent and fragmentary voice of J. P. Donleavy and tried hard to write like him.

Merton makes this suggestion to college journalism students, though a teacher might try this exercise with elementary or middle/high school students. Have students select a nonfiction author whose work they admire and write something in that voice. Try this with at least two writers. But such exercises alone will not be enough to help students find voice in their own writing. A writer still needs sustained time to write his own work in his own voice.

EXPLORATORY WRITING IN NONFICTION

In his book *Writing to Learn* William Zinsser makes a fascinating distinction between two kinds of nonfiction writing. Type A writing transmits information; the writing has authority and expertise. Type A writing is the kind of prose teachers expect in students' finished reports or final essays. But Zinsser argues that such writing can exist only if it is supported by a great deal of Type B, or exploratory, writing. Type B writing might include learning logs, interview questions on a subject, hypotheses or guesses, diagrams, notes, maps, or informal outlines.

"Our students should be learning a strong, *unpretentious* prose that will carry their thoughts about the world they live in," Zinsser writes (italics mine). In other words: writing with voice. One reason students' nonfiction so often sounds awkwardly formal and pretentious may be that we are rushing our students too quickly from Type B writing to Type A writing. We ask them to write as experts on a subject before they have digested their ideas, before they are ready. No wonder their nonfiction writing often sounds stilted.

When I was a professional freelance writer, it used to take me roughly five working days to write a feature article. The first four days I'd spend reading through other articles on the subject, taking notes, generating questions and conducting interviews, and revising those questions. Unfortunate friends got dragged to the local pastry shop (my treat) so I could tell them what I'd been learning. I was trying to get comfortable with all the new material: I needed time to talk about it until I could hear myself speaking naturally, with voice. On the fifth day I sat down to do my Type A writing, to write as an authority. On most occasions, the finished article came quickly and easily.

Teachers might think of different ways students can include exploratory writing when working on their nonfiction. Such Type B writing should include not just what the experts say on a subject but also what *you* notice, what awes or appalls you. When Jessica, a third grader, wrote a report about the mitral valve prolapse of the heart, she began by doing research. Her notes reveal not just what she has learned but also her visceral reaction to the material:

> For one white blood cell—500 red cells.
> Healthy heart, blood pumps in and out. Unhealthy heart, blood drips out of heart.
> Hearts are pretty grose.
> Never become a doctor.

Jessica's first draft conveys a sense of her fascination with this condition.

> The heart is hollow and it weighs one pound. The heart sounds like this: Labump Labump. Micravalve prolapse goes like this: shushushushushu. The heart's blood pumps in and out but the michravalve's blood doesn't pump right. Hearts are icky. If I were you I wouldn't want to be a doctor. I think I should mention that for one or two of the white blood cells there's 500 red blood cells. The heart has alot of fat, the heart even has quiticells. The quiticells look like a fat toob. The quiticalls help the heart stay in its place. The blood is really blue until ozygen hits it. When oxygen does hit it the blood turns red.

Before Jessica wrote her final draft, her teacher challenged her to take out all the "I" statements but still try to keep the lively voice of the piece intact. Here is Jessica's final draft:

> Do you know about the heart? If no, Labump, Labump, Labump!! That's how a heart sounds. By the way, a heart is hollow, believe it or not. The heart even weighs one whole pound. Can you imagine? One pound in your body. Think how much the rest of your body weighs. It must weigh a lot because a heart is really small. In the *HEALTHY* heart's body, blood

pumps in and out with no blood dripping. But if you have a Michravalve prolapse, the heart doesn't work right. The blood *does* pump but the blood drips. It's okay though. It's not something really bad. Anyway, this is how the blood drips. There are also two long tubes in your body. When the blood pumps into the heart, two tubes close tightly so the blood cleans and goes through the body. If the tubes didn't close, you will have dirty blood. With the Michravalve Prolapse, the tubes don't close tightly, blood drips out.

G. K. Chesterton once said: "If something is worth doing, it is worth doing badly." This is one of my favorite aphorisms, and one I live by when I teach writing. It seems to me vastly more important that a student try a new technique in her writing, and use it imperfectly, than never try the technique at all.

When a student is trying something new (trying to breathe voice into a feature article about Peru), we must adjust our expectations accordingly. Will upper-grade students need guidance in finding an appropriate voice? No doubt. Still, in such writing I personally prefer too much voice than too little.

Voice is far more than passion or charm; it is central to the learning process. Bill Martin said that to really own information, to truly enter into the life of a story, poem, or novel, a child must take the words of the text and transform those words in some way. When students write with voice, they put the indelible stamp of their personalities on the information they are learning—they make it their own.

Seven

BEGINNINGS

It's a funny thing about mothers and fathers. Even when their own child is the most disgusting little blister you could ever imagine, they still think that he or she is wonderful.

—ROALD DAHL, *Matilda*

OVER THE LOUDSPEAKER, the principal was droning on about bake sales, bus schedules, and permission slips. It was nine o'clock Monday morning; the fourth graders were pulling papers out of writing folders. Kids were chatting quietly, looking at stories-in-progress, trying to jump-start language that had been sitting cold for two days. Other kids faced the empty page. You could feel a serious silence inhabiting the classroom. One boy looked up, motioning to me with his eyes. He was bigger than the other kids, with dark scholarly glasses and a florid complexion that made me wonder if perhaps he was not wound a bit too tight. His first question seemed to confirm this suspicion.

"Mr. Fletcher," he said, "what if it's important to start it just right at the beginning? *Exactly* right. I mean, how do you do that?"

Automatically I answered: "Don't worry about getting it perfect at the beginning. Don't get hung up on that. When I start writing I just try to get my ideas down. Later on I figure I can always come back and fix up the beginning."

But Brian shook his head. "You don't understand. I don't think you have any idea what I'm talking about."

Another perfectionist, I thought to myself as he sighed, closed his eyes, dropped his head. He held that pose while I started moving around the classroom, talking to other kids. Ten minutes later I noticed that Brian was writing. Curiously, I went to sneak a look at his paper.

MY ADOPTION

You would usually be born from your own mother's stom-ach, but not me. I was adopted. I was born from a teenager's stomach.

I stopped to reread those lines. Brian looked up shyly while I continued reading.

My birth mother wanted to put me up for adoption but my birth father was having a hard time giving me up. During the time when he was thinking, I had to go to a different family. They took good care of me. My birth father finally made up his mind. His idea was to put me up for adoption. The family who adopted me was Carole and Sam. . . . If I wasn't adopted, my teenage family wouldn't have had enough money for me. If I stayed with them my name would have been Harvey.

In the sixth century BC Lao Tzu famously wrote: "A journey of a thou-sand miles must begin with a single step." These words apply to journeys, love affairs, careers, as well as the act of writing itself. The first word, sentence, paragraph, or passage—commonly called the *lead*—represents the author's first step toward finishing a piece of writing. But the lead is more than the first step toward getting somewhere; the lead is an integral part of the somewhere itself. The lead gives the writer his first chance to grapple with the subject at hand.

Most writing is a conceptual double helix. The author writes for herself and she writes for her audience. The twin demands of inner self and exter-nal audience chase one another throughout the process of writing the story, poem, article, or play. The lead represents the author's first crack at that dual-pronged spiral of intention.

THE DRAMATIC LEAD

It's impossible to deny the power of a beginning like Brian's. His first three sentences freeze the blood, make you sit up straight. Their simple honesty seems distilled from a self-knowledge rarely found among children, or among writers of any age. Brian's story recalls a story by another fourth grader.

WHEN I GET INTO TROUBLE

Whenever I got into trouble, my mother always had a straight look at me. I would start to cry then, not out loud but in my heart.

She goes on to describe the beatings she received from her mother. When I read the story now I find myself returning to that remarkable lead, the "straight look" her mother gave her coupled with the insight that crying begins not out loud but in one's heart. A beginning like hers grabs the reader by the throat and won't let go. Such intense honesty fuses us with the author's fate, making it impossible not to finish reading.

I tried a similar kind of lead in a story "The Christmas That Wasn't," which begins:

"In 1974 my family canceled Christmas."

Improbable words, but true. My brother Bob had been killed in a car accident in late October; we had no patience for the holiday festivities. Four days before Christmas, we packed the car and drove to a resort in the Poconos where we stayed until the holidays were over and we could come home. We quarreled, bickered, had a miserable time. Survived. A few years later I would develop this story into my first novel, *Fig Pudding*.

But such leads don't always represent the penultimate way to begin a piece of writing. It is less important for a writer to find a sensational beginning than to find the *right* beginning, the appropriate lead for that article or story. Beyond the show-stopping leads described above there are many workable ways of beginning a piece of writing. I'd estimate that eighty percent of student stories I read kick off with the words *When* ("When I was little, my father used to . . .") or *One* ("One day my grandfather took me up to the attic and showed me . . ."). Writing teachers can make students aware of the many other options available. Trying different leads can be a simple, relatively painless way for young writers to begin seeing their drafts as tentative and changeable.

STARTING IN THE MIDDLE OF A SCENE

Many writers look for a potent dose of *immediacy* to begin their writing. You can achieve that sense of here-and-nowness by starting in the midst of a dramatic scene. This has the effect of throwing the reader pell-mell into the action, diving into the frigid lake waters instead of tiptoeing in. Readers either sink or swim; usually, they survive.

The writer may decide to begin with a sound effect. This kind of lead ("Crash! The baseball smashed into the big bay window . . .") has become overused in some writing classrooms; still, raw auditory clues are an intriguing way of hooking the reader. Katherine Paterson uses this technique to begin *Bridge to Terabithia*:

> Ba-room, ba-room, ba-room, baripity, baripity, baripity, baripity—Good. His dad had the pickup going. He could get up now.

Such beginnings are often sparked by spoken dialogue. The human voice has an alluring, insistent appeal:

> "Where's Papa going with that axe?" said Fern to her mother as they were setting the table for breakfast. (*Charlotte's Web* by E. B. White)

> "Yes," said Tom bluntly, on opening the front door. "What d'you want?" (*Goodnight Mr. Tom* by Michelle Magorian)

> "Did Mama sing every day?" asked Caleb. "Every single day?" (*Sarah, Plain and Tall* by Patricia MacLachlan)

Leads like these prick the nearly universal human desire to eavesdrop on juicy conversation. Having overheard a tantalizing glimpse into people's lives, readers find it difficult to put down the book.

LEISURELY LEADS

The word on leads is that they should be short. Punchy. Dramatic. Right? Not necessarily. A lead is designed to give the reader entry; often it clues the reader into what kind of writing is at hand. A thoughtful essay might start with a slow, ruminating beginning as the writer tries to nail down some philosophical axiom. An anecdotal piece about Barack Obama might begin with a long story. Writers often decide not to jump into the thick of the plot but to begin more slowly with a description of a place, a feeling, or with a rambling introduction to the narrator or main character. Such a lead might meander through several paragraphs or even pages. Natalie Babbitt's *Tuck Everlasting* begins with a striking, if oblique, image that sets an oppressive mood for the story that follows:

> The first week of August hangs at the very top of summer, the top of the live-long year, like the seat of a ferris wheel when it pauses in its turning. The weeks that come before are only a climb from the balmy spring, and those that follow a

drop to the chill of autumn, but the first week of August is motionless, and hot. It is curiously silent, too, with blank white dawns and glaring noons, and sunsets smeared with too much color. Often at night there is lightning, but it quivers all alone. There is no thunder, no relieving rain. These are strange and breathless days, the dog days, when people are led to do things they are sure to be sorry for after.

Mary, an eighth grader, has written the following lead to a story, which deliberately does not "get to the point." She begins indirectly, using a mixture of description and philosophical reflection:

From the overcast grey sky fell tiny white snowflakes which fluttered this way and that until finally settling on some unfortunate leaf. Inevitably, the leaf would give out, and launch hundreds of tiny snowflakes down onto the sledding ground where all would be smushed together and lose their unique identity. Finally, they would all be forgotten as they were assimilated by the thawing soil. A privileged few would be lucky enough to be carried back up into the clouds.

"What happens when things die?" I thought curiously as I gazed out the back window of our station wagon. In front, Mom was saying something about being careful not to wrinkle our dresses. My dad would joke about my mom being a worry wart. Everyone would pretend to laugh and be cheerful. Gradually, the laughter subsided to nothing, leaving everyone fidgeting and self-conscious. The tension was unbearable. Only the annoying static crackle of the soft radio broke the deadly silence. We were on our way to my grandmother's funeral.

Most novice writers would have begun much more simply, perhaps with the last sentence. Mary's lead has a reflective tone; it also builds suspense for what will follow.

BEGINNING AT THE ENDING

A writer can turn a story on its head by starting at the ending and explaining how such an ending came about. Such leads play with time in a way that can be startling, even disorienting, to the reader. A journalist will often begin with a surprising, provocative argument and proceed to systematically lead the reader through the logic and evidence that warrants such a conclusion. The strategy can also be used dramatically by narrative writers and poets. Arthur Yorinks' outrageous picture book, *Louis the Fish,* begins:

> One day last spring, Louis, a butcher, turned into a fish.
> Silvery scales. Big lips. A tail. A salmon.

The author then takes us back to explain how Louis turned into a fish. Knowing how the story will end, the reader experiences Louis's transformation not with a sense of surprise but with a sense of satisfaction and inevitability at how the story reaches its conclusion.

INTRODUCING THE NARRATOR

Sometimes a writer designs the lead to introduce the character who will, in turn, tell the story. Readers who can connect with the narrator will continue reading. Certain narrators introduce themselves boldly. *Moby Dick's* famous first sentence ("Call me Ishmael") reaches out to us like a handshake: hearty, masculine, intimate. We can trust this man and the way he reports the story. We will listen.

Perhaps no narrator was bolder than Walt Whitman in his epic poem *Leaves of Grass,* which begins:

> *I celebrate myself,*
> *And what I assume you shall assume,*
> *For every atom belonging to me, as good belongs to you.*

Writers often use a sprinkle of humor to introduce their narrators. Humor relaxes the writer and helps insure that the writing will have voice; moreover, a narrator who can make us chuckle quickly begins to earn our trust. Marjorie Sharmat's *Gila Monsters Meet You at the Airport* begins with the narrator, a boy who announces:

> I live at 165 East 95th Street, New York City, and I'm going to
> stay here forever. My mother and father are moving. Out West.

Certain narrators are anything but trustworthy. At the beginning of the story, these characters seduce us with all sorts of tricks, twitches, and outrageous claims. In a story with an *unreliable narrator,* the author creates a tension between the "true" story and the narrator's peculiarly one-sided perception of that truth. This tension helps pull the reader through the narrative. Poe's short story "The Tell-Tale Heart" begins with a man on the brink of madness speaking to us in a voice choking with feverish paranoia:

> True!—nervous—very, very dreadfully nervous I had been
> and am; but why *will* you say that I am mad?

He explains that he had developed his hearing to the point where he could hear "all things in heaven, most things in hell." The perfect man to relate the bloody tale that follows.

The True Story of the Three Little Pigs, by Jon Scieszka, provides an example of an unreliable narrator that is accessible to children of all ages. The lead sets the tone for the book.

> Everybody knows the story of the Three Little Pigs.
> Or at least they think they do. But I'll let you in on
> a little secret. Nobody knows the real story, because
> nobody has ever heard *my* side of the story.

In this hilarious picture book the big bad wolf finally gets a chance to set the record straight. Alexander T. Wolf uses all the tricks of the unreliable narrator—humor, logic, appeals to sympathy, chumming up to the reader—as he tells his side of the story. I am not a murderer, he insists throughout this book; I have been monstrously misunderstood. The humor and subtleties of this book will best be appreciated by older students and adults.

Bruno Bettelheim argued the merits of reading children the undiluted versions of the classical fairy tales. I heartily agree. But children familiar with the original version of "The Three Little Pigs"—and who isn't—will be delighted at the wolf's transparent attempts at revisionist history.

Writing is not an exact science. One problem with a book like this is that it may encourage the categorizing and dissection of literature at the expense of the whole. Readers might get the notion that all possible leads must fit into the five or six options suggested in this chapter.

This is dangerous. There are many different ways to begin a story, article, poem, or play. Some writers begin with an intriguing generalization, a statement that provides a backdrop for the rest of the work. Such a generalization (a close relative of the thesis statement in expository writing) may suggest a central theme for what follows. Melissa, a fourth grader in Brooklyn, begins her story, "My Dog:"

Once in your life you get a best friend. Well, maybe twice. But anyway, mine was a dog. A beautiful, gray-black, glassy-eyed, curly wurly tailed, fat Norwegian Elkhound. She was beautiful.

Other strategies for leads include:

- *Question:* "Did you know that the sucking power of an infant is five times as strong as the sucking power of an adult?"
- *Intriguing detail:* "My parents met in Saigon in 1968, the Year of the Snake."
- *Sentence fragments.* "A 42 year old man. A man of heart and soul." Or: "Expensive furs. Blubber and oil."

A tenth-grade student began his story thus: "My mother always used to say the cat had an alarm clock in his stomach, so when he didn't show up for dinner one night people started getting nervous . . ."

In which category does this lead fit? I don't know. I do know that it makes me want to continue reading. When writing works, it works. Maybe we should leave it at that.

THE MISLEADING LEAD

Michael, a first grader, reads his book to the class.

"I have a farm," he says. "It has lots of animals." (He turns the page.) "Fooled ya! It's a toy farm!"

The children gasp, burst into laughter.

"Read that again!" one boy pleads.

Michael beams and starts rereading his book from the beginning.

Writers who explore powerful, personal subjects often begin with a "blurting lead" that tells too much too fast: "Last summer Gilly, my pet guppy, had fifty-three babies. . . ." Such leads give away the punch line of the narrative. They rob the reader of the chance to be shocked by the story in the same way the writer was shocked by the actual event.

The *misleading lead* is one way to set up and protect the surprise element in a piece of writing. Such a beginning withholds information from the reader and gives only the faintest kind of foreshadowing for the events to come. We are on tricky ground here. Writers should be very careful about withholding information. The reader may feel cheated, manipulated, and stop trusting the writer. But when the misleading lead is skillfully handled it can be a nifty way to begin a piece of writing. Take the following beginning by Pat Zibulsky, an elementary school teacher from Great Neck, New York:

> What a joy to be the lucky parent of an only child! We laugh together. We sing songs. We enjoy running mundane errands. We splash at the pool. We engage in delightful, intelligent conversation.
>
> Eight-year-old Julie has been an only child since her older sister Jamie went off to camp last week. Our normally turbulent household has settled into a peaceful rhythm....

Or take the following lead to a widely anthologized short story:

> The morning of June 27th was clear and sunny, with the fresh warmth of a full-summer day; the flowers were blossoming profusely and the grass was richly green.

Thus begins "The Lottery" by Shirley Jackson. From this idyllic start, the story proceeds to gradually unveil a horrific ritual—human sacrifice taking place in a small rural American town.

THE AMBIGUOUS LEAD

Many of us, taking a cue from William Zinsser, among others, have exhorted students to write clearly. One writing teacher told his students: "A story beginning has to be clear—you have to take the reader firmly by the hand and lead him in. You don't want your reader to get confused. Or worse: lost."

This advice is useful, but not universally true, either. A skilled writer will often use a teasing flash of ambiguity, a purposeful lack of clarity, to seduce the reader. Gwen, a fifth grader in Saratoga, New York, begins her story this way:

> From behind a tree, I saw a man-like figure lumber into the forest.

Is it a man? Or is it something else? We race ahead to find out. Mark, a fourth grader, also uses an ambiguous lead:

> In most ways I am just like other kids my age.

We read on to discover that Mark has Tourette's syndrome. The key word, of course, the word that makes it impossible for me to stop reading is "most."

The following essay of mine begins with an ambiguous lead. The key word is the unspecified "it" in the first sentence.

THE FIRST SHAVE IS THE CLOSEST

Girls know it when they get their first period. As a boy I remember watching TV with my family when my sister suddenly stood up, blushing, and ran to the bathroom with Mom close behind.

The bathroom door was shut for some time. When it opened, there was an expression on my sister's face I had never seen before. She had been gone from the living room less than an hour, but during that time an utter transformation had taken place. My mother treated her with new respect, and even my father seemed uneasy in her presence.

That evening, and for several evenings thereafter, she and my mother held long, secret talks behind closed bedroom doors. This sudden female complicity left me with only one conclusion:

Somehow, while I was watching Walt Disney on the tube, my sister had become a woman.

My transformation from boyhood to manhood was, in contrast, agonizing in its slowness. Even the leisurely swelling of my sister's breasts seemed violent compared with the almost imperceptible deepening of my voice and elongation of my bones.

Still, slow as they might be, my physical changes were terribly important to me. The thing was they never built to a sufficient peak for my father to get involved the way my mother had with my sister. My sister and I were just two years apart, but while Mom was discussing moon secrets with Elaine, Dad kept his distance from me. This worried me. I wasn't sure if I was growing up right or not.

Awkwardly, I grew through the early teens. In my sixteenth year a thin, hairy growth sprouted on my face; I was delighted when my father began to show interest in this sorry excuse for a beard. I began eagerly awaiting the day when I would get my first shave. But I was uncertain how this rite of passage would take place. Would my father give me a little booklet to read, as he had done with the Facts of Life? Or would it be something he would have to show me personally, maybe one of the few remaining rituals still physically passed down from father to son?

One spring morning my father motioned me into his bathroom and shut the door. His large presence filled the tiny room.

"I'll shave first," he told me. "You watch me and then you'll have your turn."

He needn't have said that: I'd watched my father shave dozens of times before and the process had never failed to amaze me. To watch my father shave was to witness an almost mystical transformation from beast to beauty. He began sleepy-eyed, hair in disarray, looking like a bear emerging from winter-long hibernation. Then he went to work. Shaving took him a good forty-five minutes, but when he finished his face gleamed like polished stone.

He began with an exacting pre-shave ritual: washing his hands, lathering his face, rinsing it, and then covering it over with shaving cream.

"Now you let it sit for a minute so the shaving cream can go to work softening your whiskers," he said. "You don't want to rush a good shave."

He shaved with long vertical strokes, eyes narrowed in concentration, mouth screwed up in a dazzling array of expressions—anger, pensiveness, surprise—to accommodate the razor. After finishing, he applied a second coat of shaving cream and shaved again, this time with lateral strokes. Not a single beard stalk survived this checkerboard shave. Finally, he rinsed off and applied after-shave lotion.

My turn. Mine were awkward strokes, as if I were discovering for the first time the strange shape of my face. My father's practiced hand had not left a scratch on his skin—mine was bleeding in several places by the time I had finished. He showed me how to plaster the nicks with bits of tissue paper until they closed naturally.

I ended the ritual by splashing a generous amount of after-shave lotion on my face, and experienced for the first time the surprising sting of alcohol on my tender skin.

I have shaved many thousands of times since that first shave, and my father and I have had a healthy share of father-son disagreements. But even today I still follow the shaving ritual exactly as he first taught it to me.

Nowadays I often run into guys who tell me that their fancy new razors give them the closest shaves they've ever had. As far as I'm concerned, that is just a lot of talk.

The first shave is the closest. Don't let anyone try to tell you otherwise.

Eight

ENDINGS

I think the end is implicit in the beginning. It must be.
If that isn't there in the beginning, you don't know what
you're working toward. You should have a sense of a
story's shape and form and its destination, all of which is
like a flower inside a seed.

—EUDORA WELTY

NICKI TOMARELLI was driving through Queens, New York. She had just eaten a big spicy lunch at an Indian restaurant and suddenly found herself in desperate need of a bathroom. There! A Mobil gas station! She double-parked and raced inside—both bathrooms were locked. OUT OF ORDER. Nicki looked imploringly at one of the mechanics.

"Couldn't I please . . . ? It's really an emergency."

"Sorry. The plumbing's been all gutted."

Stumbling outside, she spotted a funeral home across the street. It's come to this, Nicki said to herself, running toward it. She stepped inside and was greeted by a very tall and menacing security guard.

"May I help you?" he asked in a booming low voice. Faced with this voice and the man's looming presence, Nicki faltered, gulped.

"Yes . . . I've, uh, I've come to pay my respects," she stammered.

He gave her a brief hard look.

"This way, please." He led her down a short hallway to one of the parlors. The room was deserted but for a coffin flanked with baskets of red roses at the far end. With his eyes he motioned down to an open book.

"Sign in, please."

She signed. The guard motioned that she might approach the coffin. He flanked her as she walked. The coffin was a great gleaming gold thing. The dead man was reassuringly old, white-haired, and unremarkable. Nicki knelt and began to pray, apologizing profusely to God, and threw in a few good words for the deceased man's immortal soul as well. All the while, she could feel the guard's eyes on the back of her neck. She stood up and moved to the back of the room. The guard was still looking at her.

"May I use the restroom?" Nicki asked as calmly as she could manage.

"Certainly," he replied. "Down that corridor on the right."

A few minutes later she was back on the streets, breathing huge sighs of relief. She had survived.

Exactly one month later a check arrived in the mail. The check was made out to Nicole Tomarelli in the amount of five thousand dollars. It turned out that the deceased man in the funeral parlor had specified in his will that any person who attended his wake was to be given a gift in that amount. The astounded woman contacted her lawyer. He laughed and suggested Nicki deposit the check. She did; the check cleared.

Books about writing devote a great deal of time to leads, transitions, organization, but very little time to the finale: the end. For expository writing, students are often advised to carefully restate what has already been said. But the ending is far more than the final ribbon that adorns a piece of writing, the rhetorical hairspray to keep everything in place. The ending may well be the most important part of a piece of writing. It is the ending, after all, that will resonate in the ear of the reader when the piece of writing has been finished. If the ending fails, the work fails in its entirety.

A basic question all writers must grapple with: What's the best way to end my poem, story, article, play, or novel? Consider this brief narrative by an eighth-grade girl:

THE GIRL

A girl sitting alone in the cafeteria drinking her tears away while immature girls are throwing food. The girl is too scared to fight back. All she can do is ignore them.

They surround her and make her feel miserable but they don't care. I guess those girls just don't have feelings because they are immature brats. They make the girl feel sometimes that life is not worth living if this is how it is going to be.

Nobody has to take this abuse. But she does and is so scared to fight back that she goes away crying while these kids are cracking up in her face.

There are immature brats everywhere. Some are in this school. Maybe you are one of them in this story. Maybe I am the girl sitting alone in the cafeteria. Just maybe.

I like her ending—it carries the smell of sweet revenge. She strikes back at her tormentors and pays her way with honesty and courage. This ending, like the ending to the funeral-home anecdote that begins this chapter, is a *surprise ending*. (I would have used a sub-heading, but it would have spoiled the surprise!)

O. Henry, the short-story writer, made a living on surprise endings. (See "The Gift of the Magi," among others.) Readers delight in the ol' switch-eroo, the impossible shocker ("His *wife* killed her?!"), that thrill we get when our expectations get violated at the last minute. Surprise endings are a fine and honorable way to conclude a story, film, or play.

But surprise endings are difficult to pull off. Too often, the surprise ending feels trite, contrived. A good surprise ending should never feel arbitrary; in fact, the author will quietly plant the seeds to such an ending early in the writing for the perceptive reader to discern.

"The most wonderful stories, the ones that stick with you forever, are stories with endings that are both surprising and inevitable," says Jane Yolen. "But in order to surprise the reader, first the author has to be surprised by what happens. Sometimes you think you know what the ending will be, but when you get to the ending it's not there."

The writer does not necessarily aim to construct an ending to make the reader gasp (or gag). Rather, the writer tries to marry the right ending for the writing. We can help our students improve their endings by first helping them become aware of the various kinds of endings available to them.

THE CIRCULAR ENDING

In classical Greek mythology, the hero or heroine starts at home, goes out into the world, struggles to overcome great obstacles, acquires wisdom and knowledge through experience, and returns home again. This cycle of flight and return is a central pillar of literature. The main character—Ulysses in *The Odyssey,* Meg in *A Wrinkle in Time,* Max in *Where the Wild Things Are*

—discovers that you can come home again, though you will find yourself changed by the journey.

Cynthia Rylant's *The Relatives Came* begins with the relatives leaving Virginia before sunrise. After a long journey, they meet their northern kin and commence a few weeks of "hugging and eating and breathing together." The time finally comes when the relatives—now richer, fuller, and happier—must leave for their journey back to Virginia. They drive home and go to bed thinking of the next summer. The circle is complete.

The Ghost-Eye Tree, by Bill Martin Jr., also has a circular structure reminiscent of Greek myths. A brother and sister leave the safety of their house one night to fetch a bucket of milk. On the way to and from Mr. Cowlander's, the milkman, they must pass the dreaded "ghost-eye tree." The two children survive their ordeal, conquering the demons of fear and the unknown. The safety and solidity of "home"—their house and mother—take on a new significance by the end of this book.

"Poem" by Langston Hughes provides a simple, moving example of a circular ending:

Poem

> *I loved my friend.*
> *He went away from me.*
> *There's nothing more to say.*
> *The poem ends,*
> *Soft as it began—*
> *I loved my friend.*

In a piece of writing with a circular structure, the reader encounters the ending-as-beginning but not with a sense of "This is redundant—I read this earlier." Rather, a well-written circular ending gives the reader a second chance to encounter important material or a crucial detail that might otherwise be glossed over on the first reading. In this way it allows the reader to grasp the significance of the beginning for the first time. I suspect that T. S. Eliot may have been getting at something like this when he wrote these famous lines in his *Four Quartets:*

> *We shall not cease from exploration*
> *And the end of all our exploring*
> *Will be to arrive where we started*
> *And know the place for the first time.*

THE AMBIGUOUS ENDING

Stories cry out for resolution. We demand to know who wins and who loses, who dies and who lives happily ever after, whom she marries and whom she spurns. Yet some writers toy with this expectation, deliberately withhold this resolution, and leave the reader twisting in the wind. I have ambivalent feelings about the ambiguous ending; it can infuriate the reader and should be used sparingly. Still, it can be a potent tool.

Perhaps the most famous example of this kind of unresolved finale is "The Lady, or the Tiger?" a short story most students don't encounter until eighth or ninth grade. A young princess has had a love affair with a young man far below her station. When this affair has been found out, the young man is brought before the king, who orders the young man to an arena. Two doors face him, one with a lovely young woman behind it, the other with a ferocious tiger. He glances up. His lover, the princess, knows which is which. She looks down and gives him a signal. . . .

An ambiguous ending more accessible to young children can be found in *Granpa,* a spare picture book by John Burningham that chronicles a number of small moments between Granpa and his granddaughter Emily. Throughout the book, Granpa is identified with a green chair. Near the end of the book we find Granpa sick, sitting on this chair with blanket and medicine beside him. The last page shows the girl staring at the empty chair.

In the classroom this book prompts a variety of responses. Many kids look up with quizzical expressions. What happened? Where did he go? When I can force myself not to explain the ending, or push my own interpretation onto the children, a rich discussion often ensues.

"I think he's dead."

"Yeah, my grandpa died two years ago."

"No, he's not dead. He just went upstairs."

"I bet he went back to Florida. That's where my grammy and poppa live."

I make a point of agreeing with any plausible response. If we take seriously Louise Rosenblatt's transactional theory of literature, we must allow students to bring their own histories and experiences to make sense of a book like this. Teachers should resist the urge to impose the "correct" interpretation to any poem or book. Burningham's ending exasperates some readers, but others find it roomy and liberating. The author has created a space large enough for different readers to climb inside it, to make it their own. An ambiguous ending like this one will challenge the reader to take a more active stance toward the book, to imbue the story with the reader's own personal meanings; it will also require students to be able to defend their interpretations.

Jeannie Baker uses a hauntingly ambiguous ending in her book *Where the Forest Meets the Sea*. With a mixture of realistic details and fantasy, Baker brings alive the world of the Australian rain forest. The final two pages offer two very different visions for this rain forest's future: pristine wilderness or a developed resort complete with television and motels. The book ends with a haunting question—"But will the forest still be here when we come back?"—that asks students to choose between these two futures.

THE POIGNANT ENDING

How to end. Leave them laughing or crying? A small detail? A funny remark? A visual image to linger in the reader's mind?

Robert, the main character in John Steptoe's *Stevie*, spends most of the book complaining about the pesty little boy he must watch. When Stevie finally leaves, Robert begins thinking of all the fun times he and Stevie had together. The book ends with Robert pondering Stevie over his bowl of soggy corn flakes:

> He really wasn't so bad.
> He was kinda like a little brother.
> Little Stevie.

At the end of *Charlotte's Web* Wilbur reminisces about Charlotte. It takes a hard-hearted reader to resist being moved by the final paragraph:

> Wilbur never forgot Charlotte. Although he loved her children and grandchildren dearly, none of the new spiders ever quite took her place in his heart. She was in a class by herself. It is not often that someone comes along who is a true friend and a good writer. Charlotte was both.

This ending leaves a sharp emotional residue that stays with the reader when the book has been finished. It concludes with an observation by the author, a realization by the main character, to pull together the final strands of the story. A sixth grader in New York uses this technique in his story: "A Time When I Learned the Parent's Love." (See Figure 8-1.)

Figure 8-1

A Time When I
Learned the Parents Love

When I was living in Korea
I lived with my grandmother.
One day my teacher told me
that we were gonna have a test next
week. But I didnt study that
day because I thought the
teacher would give us an easy
test.
Next days I told my
grandmother about having a
test. Then my grandmother's
face turned red and said
"You better study a lot and
fast." But I didnt listen to

her. I just played baseball.
Next weeks when I got
the test. I was very surprise
because the test was very hard

Figure 8-1 *(continued)*

I felt that I was very stupid to think that the test would be easy.

The result of the test was 52. My grandmother hit my leg 10 times with stick when she saw the score. My leg hurted very much, but my feeling hurted much more.

That night when I was sleeping, I felt something or someone touching my red striped leg. When I opened my eyes a little, I saw my grandmother crying. I think she felt sorry for me, and didn't wanted to hit me. I was very happy to know that my grandmother cared me. And I felt this sudden feeling, I think it was the parents' love.

Poignant endings can be quite powerful. In certain cases, the ending is absolutely crucial to understanding the work as a whole. Such endings work as the last piece of a jigsaw puzzle, without which the whole would feel incomplete.

Among published authors, Charlotte Zolotow is a master of endings. In many of her books, the various threads of the story are not woven into any coherent fabric until the very last page. In *A Father Like That,* the story begins with a boy sitting with his mother, lamenting his missing father:

> I wish I had a father.
> But my father went away
> before I was born.

Throughout the book, the boy imagines all the fun he and his father would have: playing checkers, telling jokes, visiting school during Parents' Night. The first time I read this book, I wondered how Zolotow could possibly end it. If the father did come back, it would feel like a cheap, tacked-on happy ending. If the father did not return, I would be left feeling sad. But the author finds an honest ending through the character of the mother. She listens patiently to her son and, on the last two pages, reminds him:

> "I like the kind of father
> you're talking about.
> And in case he never comes,
> just remember
> when you grow up,
> you can be
> a father like that yourself!"

THE IRONIC ENDING

We find ourselves in pretty deep water when we talk about irony, particularly with young writers. Irony is a highly sophisticated technique that lies well beyond the abilities of most young writers (or adult writers, for that matter). Irony is a figure of speech in which the actual intent is expressed in words that carry the opposite meaning. Ironic writing is characterized by restraint and understatement—a coolness in expression when the writer's emotions appear to be most heated.

Irony can be a devastating device used at the end of a poem or story. George Orwell's bleak totalitarian novel *1984* ends with the bullet entering Winston Smith's head and the sentence: "He loved Big Brother."

In the final two pages of Toni Morrison's searing and painful novel *Beloved,* the author repeats a sentence three times: "It was not a story to pass on." This strikes me as hugely ironic: When I finished that novel I felt an overwhelming need to do just that, to share the book with friends, to tell the story, to pass it on.

I often try ironic endings in my poetry, such as this poem about a man's doomed and delusionary feelings for a toll booth woman he encounters each morning en route to work. Is the ending too cute? Too pat? You decide.

Toll Booth Woman

I am in love with a toll booth woman.
She doesn't know it.
It is a simple affair
Strictly ruled by numbers.
I spend ten seconds with her each morning.
She demands nothing of me
Except a single silver coin.
I reach out to touch her hands:
They are always cold.
Once I brought her some gloves.
She thanked me but said
She needed her fingers bare.
Once I told her a little story—
It took me five days
To finish.
Once she broke a twenty for me
And once she broke my—what?
Faith? Heart? You decide.
I know her kind eyes have seen it all,
Princes, politicians, and priests

All reaching up to her
With money stuffed in their fists.
Yet I believe she knows who I am.
I'm the one who risks his life,
Sliding across six lanes of rush-hour traffic,
Fighting to get to her priceless
Twenty-five cent smile.

Nine

TENSION

*If I write what you know, I bore you;
if I write what I know, I bore myself, therefore
I write what I don't know.*

—ROBERT DUNCAN

IN HIS BOOK *Heroes,* Joe McGinniss goes in search of the American hero
in order to uncover the mystique, the quintessential qualities of courage
and leadership that drive such men and women. At one point McGinniss
goes to the home of William Styron, author of *Lie Down in Darkness.* The
two men stay up late drinking and talking. Bedtime. Styron tells McGinniss to make himself at home, have whatever he wants for breakfast in the
morning except for one thing, a can of Maryland crabmeat, very special
crabmeat, which Styron has been hoarding for a very special occasion.

Next morning, while William Styron is still asleep, McGinniss gets up
early. Despite the late hour of the previous night, McGinniss is feeling fit,
in high spirits. He bounds downstairs, goes into the kitchen, and makes a
beeline for that last can of crabmeat. Opens it. He rummages around until
he finds flour, sugar, and eggs. Somehow he has gotten it into his head to
make a soufflé, a crabmeat soufflé, a dish he has never before made, never
even heard of. But the idea has inspired him nevertheless.

He goes to work, puts it into the oven. A tantalizing aroma soon begins
to fill the house. Not long after that, William Styron stumbles downstairs.
The author's initial reaction—shock, anger—quickly melts away when he
tastes that crabmeat soufflé: silky, bubbly, impossibly delicious.

This tale—a kind of twisted modern version of Eve picking the fate-
ful apple—touches an essential element of narrative: something happens.

Something changes. Something goes wrong. The protagonist or main character moves through the world, but at some point, he or she will encounter trouble, resistance. Now the story becomes interesting. This is such a fundamental expectation that while we read we are always on edge, slightly tense, awaiting the first signs of calamity. We actually get disappointed when events unfold smoothly: "Nothing is happening . . ."

Tension staples the reader's eyes to the page, and writers work hard to create it. Conflict remains the quickest way of creating instant tension. In literature, conflict (as my English 101 professor explained it) falls into three broad categories: Person versus Person, Person versus Nature, and what I will call the Inner Conflict.

PERSON VERSUS PERSON

In the classic story structure, the main character has a problem (Max gets sent to his room) that usually gets worse (he sails to a distant land where ferocious monsters menace him) before it gets any better (he scares the monsters and makes it, safely, back home again). The conflict, and the way that conflict worsens, ratchets up the tension in a story, particularly when two strong-willed people lock horns.

In many student stories, the person versus person conflict goes no further than arguing or outright physical fighting: pushing, kicking, throwing toys, etc. Such narratives tend to concentrate on the *what* and *how* of the conflict at the expense of the *why*. The reader rarely gains any insight into the root cause. We need to explore with young writers the psychological nature of human conflicts.

War with Grandpa, by Robert Kimmel Smith, explores an unusual dispute between a boy and his grandfather. The grandfather moves into the boy's house; his inability to climb stairs makes it necessary for him to take the boy's beloved bedroom on the main floor. The boy cannot understand this; he reacts angrily with guerilla war tactics—stealing the grandfather's watch, hiding the old man's shoes, etc. In this story the tension comes not merely from the clash of wills but also from the way the conflict gets played off against the boy's love and basic respect for his grandfather. We read fearing the worst, wondering if their "war" will damage that underlying layer of affection and respect.

Tight Times, a picture book by Barbara Shook Hazen, begins with a familiar conflict between a young child and parents who are unwilling to let him get the dog that he desperately wants. This initial disagreement is set amidst a background of shaky financial times—second jobs, no vacations—a bleak mood reinforced by Trina Schart Hyman's starkly effective black-and-white illustrations. Thus, the story gets fueled by several sources of tension. The initial parent-child conflict quickly gets swallowed up by a bigger problem when the boy's father loses his job.

I worked in a sixth-grade classroom in District 10, the Bronx, where all the students were boys. Their bored, canny eyes grew incredulous when I suggested they each try writing a picture book. They rolled those eyes, laughed, and flopped loudly on their desks. You hear this guy? Picture books: Ha! I was ready for this reaction and pulled out three powerful picture books. I read them aloud: *Faithful Elephants* by Tsuchiya, *Nettie's Trip South* by Ann Turner, and *Smoky Nights* by Eve Bunting.

The boys stopped rolling their eyes. They listened.

And they wrote well. The teacher (who admitted that those kids had learned only a "thimbleful" all year) and I were particularly surprised by a book by Raul, a handsome boy who was already taller than me. For me, it is the narrator's distance from the conflict—the way he tries to keep above the fray—that gives the book its charm. (See Figure 9-1.)

PERSON VERSUS NATURE

During college I spent three months in the tiny island kingdom of Tonga, South Pacific, on a foreign study program. One afternoon my college friends and I went swimming. A perfect beach in paradise. We stripped off our shirts and dove in. Immediately a strong riptide through the barrier reef started pulling us out to sea. I turned onto my back and began backstroking (my best stroke) toward the shore. Five, ten, fifteen strokes. But somehow I must have gotten turned around; when I looked up there was nothing but the indifferent vastness of water in every direction. The shore was nowhere to be seen.

Panic. I fought it off, spasm after spasm. I fought off the needling voice in my brain that kept saying: "You're gonna die." I had borrowed a pair of shorts from my friend Drew Remignanti but they were too small for me. They kept unsnapping, sliding down and tangling my legs. Three times I wasted precious energy snapping and resnapping the front. Finally, I decided to kick them off. Through the water, which was brilliant blue and deeply transparent, I could see myself. Naked. This was it. I'd been pulled so far offshore I could only glimpse palm trees and white sand when a swell lifted me up. I was scared

Figure 9-1

Figure 9-1 *(continued)*

Figure 9-1 *(continued)*

but I was equally determined: I hadn't come ten thousand miles to Tonga to drown. I had no intention of dying, not here. Not now. It was too stupid, too pointlessly ironic. No. If it came to it, I would tread water all night long.

I was an intermittent atheist, and at first I hesitated about praying. But what the heck. Hypocrisy seemed like the least of my worries: I started praying fast and hard.

After about half an hour something shifted. I felt it: the tiniest change in the water. The current had slightly loosened its grasp and no longer seemed to be pulling me out to sea. I tried a few tentative sidestrokes, easily, to conserve energy. My heart jumped: The shore was still invisible but I was definitely moving toward it. Twenty more strokes, easy, relaxed. Now I could hear a growing and continual roar, like applause in a stadium, waves smashing onto the reef ahead. And beyond the reef—land. Terra firma. I swam toward the sound.

As I neared the reef the applause swelled to a standing ovation. Approached from the back, the waves looked huge and muscular, green serpents guarding their queen. No place to go but over the top. With a shameless inner yelp (God: help), with all my money on this ride, I lurched forward on the shoulders of the most monstrous wave I could find. The wave somersaulted me forward and flattened me under several tons of water. Underwater. My breath sealed off, I surrendered to the ocean. I surfaced, gasped, and got immediately buried by a few more liquid tons. This time when I popped up I was in waist-deep water. Standing. Standing naked on coral so sharp it shredded the bottoms of my feet—I still have the scars. I cried out; I tell you I don't know if anything has ever felt so good.

A person versus nature conflict often boils down to survival: the individual's struggle to survive against fire, flood, locusts, etc. (Jack London's "To Build a Fire" is my all-time favorite story of this kind.) Unfortunately, person versus nature conflicts usually lead to blockbuster films that rely heavily on special effects: *Jaws, Jurassic Park, Titanic.* When such movies become the model for similar conflicts in student writing, the writing suffers a great deal.

William Steig's *Brave Irene* is a terrific picture book for introducing the person versus nature conflict. Irene's mother has made a dress for the duchess' ball; the girl must deliver it to the duchess. A sudden snowstorm forces Irene into a journey of near heroic proportions.

The person versus nature conflict helps to reveal the harshness of the environment. But, a more important use of such conflicts is to reveal character, to put characters into a situation that tries them almost to the breaking point.

Characters must find within themselves resources they never knew they had. In *Brave Irene,* readers will be awed by Irene's courage and tenacity as she fights against the snow, the cold, the "wounding wind." In Gary Paulsen's *Hatchet,* thirteen-year-old Brian Robeson gets stranded in the Canadian wilderness. Brian learns again and again to consider himself, his imagination, his observations, the most precious survival tools he has.

One variant of the person versus nature conflict is a character's first encounter with something new that must be reckoned with: a hornet's nest, a raw oyster, or the ordinary newness of a White Castle hamburger as described in the following story by Alison Chin, a New Jersey third grader:

THE WHITE CASTLE HAMBURGER

One night when I came home from New York City, we stopped to get some White Castle Hamburgers. We bought frozen hamburgers and some that we could eat in the car, and I never had one before. Well . . . you see, I bit in the hamburger, and it was really dark and I saw a green thing in my hamburger. I said, "Aaaaaaaaa, there is a green thing in my hamburger!" My brother (who always eats them) said: "Let me see." When I gave the hamburger to him he started laughing and said: "That's a pickle!" And then everyone started laughing.

INTERNAL CONFLICT

In the internal conflict (man versus himself, woman versus herself), the main character tries to reconcile opposing forces or desires. In Margaret Wild's powerful picture book *Fox,* a magpie with a burnt wing must choose between staying with Dog or going off with Fox, who can run faster. The choices Magpie ultimately makes will provoke rich discussion in the classroom.

In my novel *Flying Solo* several classmates wrestle with internal conflicts. Rachel, the main character, has trouble forgiving herself for being mean to Tommy Feathers, a classmate who died unexpectedly. To punish herself, she stops talking. And when Bastian learns that his family is moving to Hawaii, he must decide about what to do with Barkley, his puppy. The dog would have to be quarantined for several months, and Bastian worries about what affect this might have on the puppy. Bastian can be malicious to kids in the class, but this internal conflict helps to reveal another side of him, and makes him a more sympathetic character.

Often an internal conflict does not exist in isolation but gets connected to another kind of conflict. When I nearly drowned in Tonga as I fought to stay calm, to stay afloat, I argued with myself: Should I pray or not? As the blizzard worsens, brave Irene wonders: Should I keep going or turn back? Internal conflicts involve choice: free will. Internal struggles can produce unique forms of tension—guilt, worry, shame—as the character gets torn between conflicting impulses. Tell the police or keep it a secret? Return the wallet or keep it?

A story that turns on an internal conflict requires a great deal of honesty from the author, as in this piece by Aimee, an eighth grader:

JEALOUSY

"Dad." She called him dad. I couldn't believe it. I didn't understand. Dad??? It was one weekend where I went to my Dad's house. My step sister Carrie was there calling him Dad.

I guess I could admit the way I'm feeling about my Dad and Carrie's relationship. It's the way you feel when everyone else gets great presents but you get something worth nothing. Or when my brother got the bigger room.

I think I felt this way because she wasn't his daughter, and she was treated as if she were. I never had the joy of living with two parents, and she has her mom, my Dad, and she's loving every minute of it.

When I realized she was calling him Dad, all those feelings were running through my head. If I had the guts, I would have yelled right then and there: "He's not your father; he's mine."

Everyone tells me that he loves us both the same. Shouldn't he love me more? They also tell me to just ignore their relationship. But sometimes I think that's not the way to solve my problem. I have no solution, except to try my best not to get upset.

In the next piece, by another eighth grader, the narrator has a conflict with his coaches and, later, his father. But the most moving parts of this story involve the boy's conflicts of conscience. This gives the prose its depth and makes this much more than just another did-wrong-got-caught-got-punished story.

During a hard-working football practice, my temper started to flare and my breath started to shorten. When it was over I went into the locker room with the intention of doing something daring or beating someone up. After I got dressed, and my breath was almost gone, I went over to get a drink of water. While I was walking out the door I purposely yanked the lever down on the fire alarm to get back at the coaches. Within seconds the alarm went off and the firemen were there.

When I went outside and saw the fire trucks, I froze and did not know what to do. I did not know whether to tell the coaches or go on the bus and go home. So I took the easy way out and went home.

The next day in school I got called down to the attendance office. Not knowing someone ratted on me, I confessed that I did it. Right away the school suspended me.

That night when I got home I was so scared to face my dad. On top of everything the worst thing about it was that my father is a city fireman.

When my dad got home that night I was scared to face him. All of a sudden I heard my dad say: "What did he do? I will kill him! Where is he?" When my dad finally got me he gave me a look to kill. If it were not for my grandma, I think I would have been on the street last night.

The next morning me and my parents had a meeting with my principal. While we were in there I was wondering what was going on in my mom's mind and my dad's mind. After it was all done, the worst part came. For the first time in my life I saw my dad cry, and that really hurt me. Seeing my dad cry— that is why I am not able to forgive myself. Also by seeing him cry, I was able to learn that my dad will always love me and forgive me for this someday.

It is not unusual to find all three types of conflict in a single piece of writing. All three kinds of tension exist in *The Ghost-Eye Tree,* by Bill Martin Jr.: the boy's continuous arguments with his sister (person versus person), his frightful encounter with the "ghost-eye tree" (person versus nature), and his struggle to control his own overwhelming fear (person versus self).

All three conflicts are also present in *Gila Monsters Meet You at the Airport,* by Marjorie Sharmat, a picture book about a boy moving from the east coast to the west. The book's tension and humor spring from the boy's stubborn refusal to move, his hilarious misconceptions about the west, and his struggle to envision his future out west through the lens of the only home he knows: New York City.

I prefer "tension" to "conflict" because the term seems more inclusive. It would be hard to define a clear conflict in Cynthia Rylant's *The Relatives Came.* Yet the pull of home creates a kind of tension that builds slowly as the story progresses. The relatives keep thinking of their grapes, back home, nearly purple enough to eat. That insistent tug of home, the fact that the relatives cannot stay forever but must finally go back to their own beds several states away, lends a poignancy to the book. (That pull between two places—home and away—is the same one Dorothy experiences in *The Wizard of Oz.*) The reader feels a gentle sadness as the relatives drive away.

The writer can also create tension between two separate times—present and future, present and past. In the following narrative by Rachel, a third grader in New Jersey, the author jumps back and forth in time while writing about her dogs:

> I had two dogs: Bello and Kimmy. Kimmy was a white dog with fluffy fur. Bello was a gray and white dog with smooth fur. I remember the times they used to play together. But that day was all over.
>
> One day Kimmy couldn't walk anymore. He was deaf, too. I knew that because before when he could hear he would always come to me when I called to him.
>
> My dad once told me a story about Kimmy. Let me tell it to you: When Kimmy was a puppy someone else owned him. When she went out for a walk one day she ran into some neighbor's house and ate a whole bag of sugar!
>
> But one Friday Mom and Dad had Kimmy put to sleep. He went back where other dogs lay buried and remembered: Cinnamon, our mom's faithful dog, Kimah, our cousin's dog, and now Kimmy, the dog who was here a little while ago.

Tension might be thought of as *resistance.* A writer can create this resistance through the voice in which the piece gets written. What follows is the beginning of a story about a family's trip to Disney World. The reader might expect that such a story would be written with anticipation or childish delight. Instead, you can feel the narrator holding back from the experience. He adopts a cynical, sarcastic voice that gives this piece a pleasing bite:

> It was a calm, quiet sunny day. I lay in a field looking up at the sky with its big puffy clouds. Then chaos started. The ground was shaking and a voice was telling me to get up. I knew that voice. Suddenly a huge crack opened in the ground next to me and I fell in. I was falling down, down through the blackness.
>
> Thump! I was lying on the floor of my room, annoyed that I'd been woken up from such a nice dream.
>
> "Sean! Get up and get dressed! We're leaving soon for Florida!" my mom's voice boomed.
>
> I stood up. I felt like I had been trampled on by a herd of elephants. I got dressed and stumbled down to the kitchen for breakfast.
>
> Ah! Breakfast. The nutritious, energizing meal which gets you ready to face the world in the morning. I walked into the kitchen to see what treat awaited me. I looked at the table and saw . . . cornflakes . . . soggy corn flakes. Dismally, I ate the cereal.
>
> About twenty minutes later, after getting ready, we had packed the car and were on our way to Florida. I sat in the back seat of the car next to my ten year old brother. I was surrounded by books, comics, and toys, which would hopefully make the trip more interesting. My brother was cheerfully playing Gameboy and having a grand old time. I was just staring out the window, thinking about the trip. We were going to Disney world, three giant amusement parks pushed into one. This drive represented our two day trek to see a mouse, a duck, and a dog. . . .

Finally, the writer can draw on the inherent tension in all metaphors, which link or compare two things that do not seem to fit together, as in this striking poem by Charles Simic:

Watermelons

Green Buddhas
On the fruit stand.
We eat the smile
And spit out the teeth.

"The Boots," a poem of my own, works off the tension between two places far apart, two vastly different situations, and a central metaphor that embraces unlikely things:

The Boots

After climbing Mt. Kilimanjaro
my boots were soaked, mud-clogged,
heavy as lead. I threw them out
and slept, dreamless,
*   in the mountain's dense shadow.*

Next morning a Masai wanderer
brought back the boots: sleek and polished,
each brass fixture snapping with light.
He had stayed up all night cleaning them
(for "the pride of work" someone later said)
and would not accept any money.

I held the boots away from my heart,
the leather soft and newly oiled,
awkwardly, no longer worthy of them,
while the man kept his silence.
I had no choice:
I gave him the boots
and flew to America the following day.

Now, years later, your curtains tremble
at the harsh words we traded,
and this coagulating darkness
where you find a queasy slumber
will not let me breathe.
I can just make out your frail spine,
the vertebrae ghostly in this dim light,
rising reluctant with each troubled breath.
You once said we all go to bed dirty,
*   and wake up clean.*

If you would wake right now
I would gladly stay up all night
and scrub clean our weary love
if it could be as we first knew it,
if it could once more be winged and fluid.
For I cannot trust indifferent sleep
to heal such deep and deliberate wounds.

Ten

A Sense of Place

*Sense of place is the sixth sense, an internal compass and
map made by memory and spatial perception together.*

—REBECCA SOLNIT

PARAMUS, NEW JERSEY: a consuming landscape. No less than five
giant malls within a one-mile radius from my desk. A great place to buy
furs, furniture, bathroom fixtures, if not exactly the most nourishing environment for a writer. If you want the truth, you should know that I'm
having a great deal of trouble writing here. Not writer's block, not yet,
but something else, something perilously close. Real restlessness. Clinical
disorientation almost to the point of nausea.

These days, writing days, I decide to start by going for some air. Maybe
a brief walk will get me off on the right writing foot. (Bad pun: see what
I mean?) Breathe in the dewy spring air. Rinse the dream fragments from
my head. The lawns on my street are thick, unbelievably green, billiard-
table smooth. In the 'burbs the men tend the lawns, and you do not mess
with a guy's lawn. At 8 A.M. Wayne, the guy next door, is already at it,
burly and shirtless, trimming his hedges. This man's lawn is his grand ob-
session. His grass defies description. Imagine a Marine's closely cropped
crew cut, the blades executing a close-order drill. A lawn of near synthetic
homogeneity. The transition from his lawn to our lawn, with its various
and sundry crab grasses, is not a pretty one. On certain mornings I can
almost hear his lawn laughing at ours: haw haw haw. . . .

Wayne waves me over. I am surprised; we haven't spoken in nearly a month.
"Ever get grubs in your soil?" he asks.
"What?"
"Grubs." He squints at me.

"Well, I—"

"If you do, here's the best way to get rid of them. Feed 'em grits." He grins. "They eat the grits, and their bodies swell up. Explode. I'm telling you, works every time." He grins again. "Remember that. Grits kill grubs."

I mumble my thanks and continue walking. Not a great place to write. Very tough town for turning a phrase. Very tricky. When I used to live on Manhattan's upper West Side things were a lot easier in this regard. Writing there was a legitimate way of life. The bookstores and coffee shops were thick with novelists and freelance journalists, poets and playwrights. The joke was that if you accidentally shot off a gun you'd kill three writers. Famous writers, too. Some days I'd watch old Isaac B. Singer slowly making his way up Broadway, heading to his favorite coffee shop. Seeing that, I'd smile, gulp my own coffee, and hurry home to write.

~

The setting, or place, creates the world in which the characters live and struggle. In this world, the plot will unfold. Something will happen.

In *The Art of Fiction,* John Gardner describes good writing as a "vivid and continuous dream." This is a useful definition for all kinds of writing: bad writing is anything that jolts the reader out of that dream. The reader must make a leap of the imagination to connect his world to the world of the writer. The writer who can create a believable world, a convincing place, goes a long way toward trancing the reader into the larger world of the article, biography, poem, or story.

Young writers typically pay little attention to setting. This is true whether the writing is set in familiar terrain (backyard, attic, grandmother's house) or in an exotic locale (a trip to Montana, a panda bear lumbering up a slope in the Himalayas, Martin Luther King sitting in his prison cell in Selma, Alabama). A boy writes a story, "My Trip to Maui," but if you snipped off the title you would find very little Maui woven into the story. It could just as easily have taken place in Brooklyn, Florida, or western Massachusetts.

I usually start writing with something I know: a detail, an image, a snatch of overheard conversation, a story, person, or place. Place is an excellent starting point because places live in the deepest parts of us. In one sense, we never leave them: We soak them up, carry them around, all the various places we have known.

"It is by the nature of itself that fiction is all bound up in the local," Eudora Welty has said. "The internal reason for that is surely that feelings are bound up in places. . . . Location is the crossroads of circumstance, the proving ground of 'What happened? Who's here? Who's coming?'"

Clam digging is a world I know. I spent three long summers digging littleneck clams on the Great South Bay off southern Long Island, New York. By itself, clam digging is not enough of a story, but I might use this setting for any number of pieces of writing: poems, stories, a novel, a feature article on the disappearing baymen on Long Island.

Clamming was a tough, fascinating world. I might start trying to animate this world by describing the clamming artifacts: our Garvey (a twenty-foot-long boat with a flat deck). Rakes and tongs. The burlap bags we used to store the clams. The cull rack we used to sort salable clams from seedlings that had to be thrown back. You'd dump a pile of clams onto the rack and shake vigorously. The legal littlenecks and cherry stones would stay: the seed clams would fall through the iron bars.

Routine. We left the dock each day at 7 A.M. and worked until mid-afternoon, or later, or earlier, if we pleased. We made our own hours. We'd drive the boat a half hour into the bay, secure the anchor, take out the tongs, and begin work.

My brother Jim and I were tongers. We worked in water just eight feet deep. The clam tongs were a giant pair of scissors, two long wooden handles attached to a basket with sharp teeth three inches long. You'd stand at the edge of the deck, drop the tongs overboard while holding onto the handles, open the tongs, jam them down, work them closed, lift up, shake out the mud, listen for clams. If you heard some, you'd lift up (keeping the basket closed or you'd drop the clams), dump them onto the deck, take a short step down the boat, throw in the tongs, and start again. In this way I'd work my way down one side of the boat while my brother worked the other. We might harvest a bushel and a half in a day, maybe more. We got paid every day, cash, by the wholesalers on the dock, some of whom weren't above shorting us a few dollars if we didn't speak up. I earned around thirty-five or forty dollars each day: I had a number of teenage friends who regularly earned over a hundred dollars a day.

I would start describing this setting with my five senses.

Touch: the noon heat, the horseflies, the blisters on my hands and the salt water that made them smart. (The job wreaked havoc on the hands. Some nights I'd wake up with my hands cramped up, knotted together. My brother would have to help me pry them apart.)

Smell: the dank, rotting smell on the deck from all the muck and crabs and seaweed we dredged up from the bottom of the bay.

Sight: girls on their sailboats a few hundred yards away, a few light-years away, smugly smiling as they skimmed past en route to Fire Island.

Sound: boats droning, clammers shouting friendly obscenities at each other, the heart-stopping sound of a mother lode of clams rattling in the tong basket when you shook it up and down.

Taste: clams on the half shell, unimaginably fresh. We'd bring out lemons and Tabasco sauce. For lunch we'd eat a couple dozen clams harvested just moments before.

Odd fact #1: The veteran clam diggers, the baymen who clammed year round and not just as summer work, each had a single seagull who perched on their boats. One seagull per boat, same seagull every day. I observed a complex symbiosis between these men and their birds. The seagulls would eat the cracked clams on the deck: sometimes the men would break open clams for the seagulls. What did the baymen get back? A mascot, I suppose, and meager companionship. I greatly admired the true baymen, tried hard to befriend them, and dreamed of one day having a seagull come land on my boat. But the baymen ignored me, and so did the seagulls. My brother and I clammed alone.

Odd fact #2: Mornings, the offshore wind would usually be mild, but after lunch a fresh, cool breeze would blow out of the south. Everyone called it the "one o'clock chop." It began blowing every day precisely at one o'clock: the old-timers said you could set your watch by it. You could see the breeze roughening the glassy waters over toward Fire Island as the breeze moved toward you. When it arrived, you could watch all the boats swing around on their anchors until every one was pointing south, into the wind.

The peculiarities of clam digging, and all my experiences in that world, eventually became grist for my first young adult novel, *The One O'Clock Chop*.

In the following story, by a second grader, the author uses three of her five senses to describe a pristine setting:

> I love wild animals. and one time I went to a caben. and the caben was on a rocky slpe. every day me and my brother climbed to the very top. we edmired the gloryes vue as we listened to the morning glores sing. it was very soothing to listen to them. and it made me warm inside. so every morning we did the same. it was a brilyant way to start my day. and it put me brother in a good mood. and it made every thing good. there was a stream that shimered. and the sunlight shone beautyfuly

> on the distant sparkles. it was great to have so many wonderful things at one caben and it was better to just go alone as I looked at all the wonderful things around me and listened to the beautyful sounds. as I hung my feet in the stream it trickled over the shining rocks. it made me feel away from every thing. when it was time to go I was sad but you can't go on dreaming for ever.

This author does not let her spelling problems prevent her from taking huge risks with language. One senses a young writer working hard here as she tries on a language of beauty and awe. I also sense that this place is a haven where she can find refuge from other problems.

Jerry Watson has made a useful distinction between *backdrop* setting and *integral* setting. Backdrop setting is simply an arbitrary place in which the story takes place. Backdrop setting has little or no effect on the rest of the story. Watson says: "The integral setting, on the other hand, exerts a great deal of influence on the values, speech, and actions of characters, the movement of plot, and the presentation of theme and mood."

"Only in cheesy realistic novels are places described for their own sake," says novelist Robert Cohen, author of *Inspired Sleep*. "The setting gets described to further what the book is about—the characters, the theme. The setting is always expressive of something more than itself."

Setting can be used in many ways in a piece of writing. A brief description of a place is an excellent way to set the scene at the beginning of a piece of writing. Carson McCullers uses this technique to begin *The Member of the Wedding*. An initial description functions like a foyer in a large house; it gives the reader time to become at home, to "feel the ground" of the story before walking into the real action. I used this technique to begin the following story:

> I park my car as close as possible to the building. It is morning, biting cold; I move quickly from the car toward the school building. There is a narrow ribbon of warmth that surrounds school buildings in the winter, a sweater of heat perhaps two feet wide, fueled by heating vents, boiler steam, convection from the windows. I hug the walls trying to stay within this warm zone as I hurry to the front door.

The setting can also be a fine way to build tension in a piece of writing. I don't mean just the it-was-a-dark-and-stormy-night kind of tension, but also the taut pull (or push) between opposing forces:

I meet with teachers in the All-Purpose Room, actually a combination science and music room. Bongos and tambourines sit in uneasy proximity to pinned arachnids and pickled mice embryos. On the wall, a plaque of BUTTERFLIES FROM AROUND THE WORLD has been placed not five inches from a large and elaborate diagram showing various musical notations. As the teachers and I talk, a bitter, lacquered smell rises to my nostrils. I can't quite tell if it is formaldehyde or the gleaming varnish on that huge African drum. . . .

The setting provides the author with an excellent way to develop character. The relationship between character and the character's physical world is a complex one: the harsh American West shaped the settlers who, in turn, cut down the forests, built communities on rivers, killed buffaloes, pushed Indians off their lands. This interrelationship lies beyond the reach of most young writers. What they can understand is this: Each of us is a product of the world we live in. Botanists and zoologists tell us that a true understanding of any species requires that the species be studied not in isolation but within its native environment. The same is true for humans. The world we live in sculpts our psyches as well as our bodies. (Professional clammers tend to be barrel-chested, with huge arms and thick, weathered hands.) Jean Craighead George explores the relationship between character and physical environment in *Julie of the Wolves:*

Miyax was a classic Eskimo beauty, small of bone and delicately wired with strong muscles. Her face was pearl-round and her nose was flat. Her black eyes, which slanted gracefully, were moist and sparkling. Like the beautifully formed polar bears and foxes of the north, she was slightly short-limbed. The frigid environment of the Arctic has sculptured life into compact shapes. Unlike the long-limbed, long-bodied animals of the south that are cooled by dispensing heat on extended surfaces, all live things in the Arctic tend toward compactness, to conserve heat.

An experienced writer can uncover subtle links between a character and her setting. Not only does environment shape character but the character's emotional state also determines how she perceives the environment. The blue sky glows like some gorgeous sapphire or stretches like some dreary barren desert, depending on how we feel at that particular moment. The skilled writer will use the way in which a character perceives a setting to give the reader significant clues about that character's state of mind.

At the end of his book *The Art of Fiction,* John Gardner suggests several writing exercises. I believe such exercises should be used sparingly with children, if at all. Still, there is at least one intriguing exercise involving setting as a way to reveal a character's state of mind:

> Describe a building as seen by a man whose son has just been killed in a war. Do not mention the son, war, or the old man doing the seeing. Then describe the same building, in the same weather and at the same time of day, as seen by a happy lover. Do not mention love or the loved one.

"A sense of place" does not necessarily mean a large landscape. Place might refer to a closet, a drawer, the inside of a wallet. Consider the following description of a car's interior by Rebecca, a fourth grader, and notice how well it gets at the mood of turbulence and disarray that is really what the story is about.

> During the protest for the homeless people, we were always rushing here and there so Mom got lots of tickets for parking in the wrong places. She'd just throw them onto the floor of the car and drive away. Whenever we got in and out of the car we'd step on those parking tickets. After awhile the tickets got trampled in with all the coffee cups and spilled coffee and napkins and wrappers and newspapers on the floor of the car. Pretty soon they got so soaked you couldn't even read the date on the tickets. A little while longer and the tickets got moldy and you'd smell that moldy smell whenever you got in the car. It wasn't long before those tickets start *disintegrating* right under your feet. Finally we couldn't stand it anymore. We cleaned out the car. But that moldy smell never really went away.

Consider also the following short story by another fourth grader. This piece of writing does many things well, utilizing successive flashbacks that quickly catapult the reader back in time before returning us to the present. I am most struck by her ability to evoke the two settings in the story, and by the tension between them:

WHISPERS IN AN OPEN FIELD

Chapter One: A Frightening Event

"What!?" I couldn't believe it was happening. Here I was standing in front of millions of people (or what seemed like millions of people). My mother crying silently with her head tilted. Her small, pale fingers clutching a white lace hanky. My dad in a blue suit looked encouragingly at me. Mrs. Taylor's face streamed with tears under lace, black veil. Everyone was looking at me. Expecting "me" to say something!

"Ah . . . well . . ." What was there to say?

I'm at the moment on an altar looking into the faces of all these strange people.

My best, best, best friend, Elizabeth Taylor, had died because of me. But wait! Don't blame me. Listen.

It happened last month. Elizabeth had come over to play. Her favorite game was just to kick a ball around. It was my turn. I kicked the ball hard, too hard. It rolled into the street. I told Elizabeth to go get it and kick it back. She ran to it. As she ran, an orange car sped out of its driveway and smacked into Elizabeth. It knocked her down against the pavement! She rolled down towards a stone a little bit and stopped.

I remember the terrible screech of the car, the hideous scream I had shrieked and the sound of Elizabeth's leather jacket rubbing against the pavement. It was horrible.

Chapter Two: A Secret Place

Yes, it was true. Elizabeth was dead. The words kept ringing in my head. But there was something else that kept blinking in my brain. The field. It was a wonderful place. My favorite place in the world. Elizabeth's too. I suppose that's why we chose it. You see, when Elizabeth was alive we used to go to this open field. It was deserted, but kept very clean. The grass was always sparkling green, and in the middle of the field was a gazebo. Actually, it was only a weeping willow tree, but it "wept" to the ground, if you know what I mean.

The reason we chose it was because we needed a quiet place, a clean place, and a deserted place. A place for what? you might ask. A place where two girls could grow into friendship.

Chapter Three: Telling It All

The place was for secrets. I suppose that I will not go there any more. Elizabeth and I made an oath: "Neither of us shall go to the field without each other." I was certainly without Elizabeth. And even though the willow branches whisper on, our secrets stay protected under the spring leaves.

"Hurry, Julie!" my mother was calling. I hate to tell you where I was going. Elizabeth's . . . fune . . . funeral!

I was purposely trying to be late. I didn't want to see Elizabeth dead in a wooden box. And I didn't necessarily think Mr. and Mrs. Taylor wanted to either. So what was the point of a funeral?

"You were great, dear!" my mother said.

Gee, I thought. All I did was say: "Elizabeth meant a lot to me." I was too embarrassed to say any more. I guess I should get Elizabeth out of my mind. I'm not going to ever think about death and funerals again. But my memories will always live. The field, the secrets, the tree, the oath, the rustle of leaves. The whispers.

Eleven

A PLAYFULNESS WITH TIME

And so we beat on, boats against the current,
borne ceaselessly into the past.

—**F. SCOTT FITZGERALD,** *The Great Gatsby*

TIME-WISE, the writer faces a dual challenge: how to handle the element of time in one's writing, but on a more basic, practical level, how to find time to write.

The writer does a remarkable thing. She spends time, often a great deal of time, on something as peculiarly intangible as a poem, an essay, a stretch of prose. She works on it gradually, house-by-house, block-by-block. Over time she may build an entire city of words. For what purpose? To acquire new knowledge? Get paid? Get published? Improve her physique? Meet fascinating people? End up with a gleaming piece of art to adorn her living room? Not likely.

We may be able to envision the sudden burst of energy required to clean out the garage, to confront that friend who inexplicably never phones anymore. We may be able to imagine blowing a large sum of money on a fancy car or new extension on our house. But who can fully imagine the staggering daily investment of sheer time required to become a skilled writer?

Ideally, the writer has an abundance of time because quite often when a writer sits down to work, nothing happens. No words or ideas come forth. This sort of frustration comes with the territory. Writers learn to factor writer's block into their time.

"Over the years I've developed the self-image of a shopkeeper," the writer Amos Oz says. "Mainly it's my business to open the joint at a set time, to sit and wait. If I have customers, it's a blessed day. If I don't, well, I'm still doing my job."

Several years ago I was given that rarest of gifts: time to write surrounded by time to waste. I was invited to spend a month at Yaddo, a writer's retreat in Saratoga Springs, New York. Heaven: a giant mansion set on four hundred pristine acres. The daily ritual at Yaddo never varied. Breakfast was served from eight to nine. After breakfast each writer or visual artist picked up a lunch box and headed off to a private studio to work. We worked every day from nine until four in the afternoon. Dinner was at six. Such vast stretches of time felt disorienting and, at first, lonely; by four o'clock I'd be starving for the sound of a human voice. (There were no telephones or televisions in the studios.) But I wrote a ton. More than the absence of interruptions, it was the lack of the *threat* of interruptions that made Yaddo a place where you could really get work done.

Most of us never get to experience a Yaddo. Back on planet Earth, few people have sustained stretches of time to write. For most of us who write, or yearn to write, time remains the greatest scarcity—more than money, space, or energy.

A typical writing day. I had it all planned. I would work on this chapter from 10:00 until around 2:30. Robert would take his regular nap from 10:00 until noon. JoAnn would go to work until noon; I had arranged for a baby-sitter to watch Robert from noon until 2:30.

My plans crashed and burned. The first sweltering day of the year; Robert sweated, fussed, and refused to nap. Feeling sorry for the little guy, I caved in, drove to Toys Я Us, and bought him a little plastic Cookie Monster pool. By the time I finally got it home and wrestled it into the backyard, Robert had fallen asleep. Sleeping Robert = Prime Writing Time. But it turned out that the pool had a small hole in the bottom. I brought it back to the store and stood in three long lines, fuming, until I could finally exchange the pool for another model.

Back home, 12:35, I started writing, but got interrupted by four phone calls from different banks. We were in the process of shopping around for a mortgage; I felt compelled to take the calls. All the while I was trapped in this cliché: the grains of sand slipping through the hourglass. No time to write this chapter about time. Another unfunny joke. Finally, I started to write again, but all the while I was listening for baby Robert, sleeping Robert, a slumbering time bomb of a Robert, ready to go off at the slightest ring of the telephone or loudly closed door.

This is the perfect excuse for not writing: no time. But the real writer refuses to fall for it. Writers write. In notebooks, on napkins, at the kitchen table surrounded by dirty plates.

I know a Cambodian man who was quite poor in his youth. There was barely money for food, let alone paper. He was in love with a young woman from the neighboring village. He would get up before sunrise, sneak down to the riverbank, and write her love letters in the wet sand. She would read them when she came down to wash clothes in the river later that morning.

In our culture, relatives, visitors, spouses, children, and salespeople are famous for devaluing the writer-at-work and often feel no hesitation about interrupting the writer on the slightest pretext. Many writers compensate by becoming fanatical about protecting their time. (I heard of one man who, upon hearing his son screaming outside his office from a fairly serious head wound, tersely reminded his wife through the closed study door: "I'm not home. I'm not here. You take care of it.")

This may be going too far. But bottom line: writers write. Writers find a way to get it done. Consistency matters. *Nulla dies sine linea:* Never a day without a line. Hemingway had a daily goal of about two hundred and fifty words. That doesn't sound like all that much, but if you write two hundred and fifty words every day you'll have a completed book by the end of a year.

Donald Murray put it like this: "I am surrounded by neighbors and friends who want to write and know more than I do, have more to say than I do, are blessed with more talent than I have, but they do not yet have the writer's habits."

Of all the writer's habits, consistency may be the habit that matters most. In a classroom the teacher decides the frequency and duration of student writing time. But for young writers, handling the issue of time in the writing itself can be very difficult. From my own observations in classrooms, the problem boils down to this: Inexperienced writers are typically controlled by the element of time in their stories.

Why? JoAnn Portalupi suggests that young children may lack the language connectors ("The summer before . . ." "The next day . . .") that might allow them to shape the contours of time in their stories.

It also strikes me that timelessness is an intrinsic part of childhood. Most kids don't keep track of time. Unlike adults, children don't measure it, save it, parcel it out. A boy sorts and resorts his baseball cards, first by team, then by position, then by batting average. Hours pass: by adult standards a colossal waste of time. But children are not adults. The river of time that runs through them is deep, strong, unbroken. When I encourage my own children to make the transition from timelessness to time planfulness, I am well aware that I am asking these children to begin moving out of their childhood.

Children have trouble controlling time in their writing because they simply do not see it as an element to control. They are oblivious to it. This may be reinforced by an overemphasis on personal narratives in many writing classrooms. Too many young writers develop a narrow conception of writer-as-reporter, whose sole task is to provide a faithful recounting of events the writer has experienced. The much-maligned "bed-to-bed" story results from the writer's inability to exclude any moment, no matter how trivial, from a particular day.

Here is a crucial discovery about time for a writer: *The experience and the writing that is based on that experience are not the same thing.* The real-life subject—and the writing based on that subject—exist as two distinct entities. Often the two are only loosely linked, connected (and distorted) by the writer's imagination.

Writers who draw on their own experiences for their writing must constantly juggle the demands of what really happened (who/what/when/where/why) with what needs to happen in the piece of writing to make it work.

The distinction between *real time* and *story time* probably has certain developmental limits. It has been my experience that most first- and second-grade writers want to include complete lists of events. In a writing conference, when I suggest they focus their writing on a particular "slice of the pie," primary grade children tend to decline my invitation. But once a writer can uncouple real time from story time (perhaps in third or fourth grade) the writer can begin to perceive time as just one more element—like character or setting—that must be considered in a piece of writing.

As an alternative to linear time, we might encourage young writers to move toward a *playfulness* with time. By playfulness I mean a sense of time as the mind plays with it—fretting about a future event, dwelling on a past slight—as we move through a series of present moments during the course of a day.

I am mowing the lawn of our Lee, New Hampshire, home, just smelling the grass, enjoying the tight reverberations from the motor running up the handle to my arms and shoulders (PRESENT). When I finish the backyard, Joseph and his friend Austin set up a sprinkler and start running through it. Their squeals bring me back to one summer afternoon when I was ten (PAST) and my uncle lit off a firecracker. I was standing further back than anyone else, but a tiny piece of rock shot into my right arm. . . . Thunder rumbles (PRESENT), and I start thinking about the cookout planned for later on (FUTURE). If it rains, where on earth will everyone sit to eat? The lawnmower sputters (PRESENT): Is it out of gas?

A writer can handle time in many different ways: cutting it, bending it back, stretching it out. When trying to teach a complex element like time, writing teachers may run the risk of mentioning rather than really delving into the issue. Teachers of middle school or high school students who want to explore with students the element of time might consider a deeper exploration with:

- Examples from literature (see Appendix)
- Examples from student writing (as important as literary examples; it is my experience that a writing strategy does not become part of the class culture until students see their peers using that strategy)
- Direct instruction

LINEAR TIME

Linear, or chronological, time is the modus operandi for writers of most ages. There is nothing wrong with this; in fact, most teachers would consider *sequence* a strength in a piece of writing rather than a weakness. I see two kinds of linear time often showing up in student writing. Sometimes time does show up in a story, but it is time wound very loosely:

> We went to Chuckee Cheese and we had fun. We played lots of
> videos and I found two quarters. Then we had pizza and soda
> and cake. I helped Anthony open his birthday presents. . . .

In this kind of story, events follow one another in a kind of "and next" fashion. We might think of this as "time as backdrop." There is some evidence of sequence—in the Chuckee Cheese ritual, video games do precede the soda and pizza—though the events are not closely linked together. This is a "Greatest Hits of the Day" story, with events placed in the right order.

A more sophisticated kind of story sequence occurs when events are shown to *cause* other events, as in the following story by fourth grader Sylvia:

> As I stepped in the car crying my mother said, "It'll be fun
> in preschool." While driving to school mom explained what I
> was going to do.
> Soon-e-nuf we were there. We walked stair-by-stair and hall-
> by-hall. Then we stopped in the room. Five years olds screaming
> and jumping all around. There was a big box. I wanted to find

out what was behind the box. But I still wanted to go home. I turned back to ask mom to go home. She was running down the hall, half way to the door. MOM COME BACK! PLEASE! Now I was running after her. When I was half way down the hall I tripped. I bruised my knee but the pain didn't bother me, all I wanted was mommy to come back and bring me home. It was no use.

The teacher brang me back in the room. I sat down. Things were flying around in my head. Why did I have to fall? Why couldn't I cry louder? I was stupid. But I survived the day, and found out what was behind the box.

Sylvia's story is truly driven by sequence—events are intricately woven together. The girl is crying *because* she has to go to school. Her mother reassures her, brings her to school, and tries to sneak away. Seeing her mother leaving causes the girl to panic and, ultimately, to hurt herself. (Incidentally, the story has both a recurring detail and an ambiguous ending that seems perfect: since we never find out what is in the box, it comes to represent school itself.)

SNAPSHOTS

Readers expect sequence in most kinds of writing. Even a biography usually ends with the subject's death. But some authors violate that expectation by deliberately removing the element of time and providing the reader with nonlinear *snapshots* of a particular world, place, or character.

In Cynthia Rylant's first book, *When I Was Young in the Mountains,* a girl reflects on her childhood memories of Appalachia. The element of time is largely absent in this book, though it does lurk in the background. We know that events in the book happened in the past. And some pages are linked together (first the children heat water for their bath—later they shiver as they drink hot cocoa). But most events in the book are removed from any kind of linear sequence. The very lack of sequence gives this book its timeless quality and charm.

The writing of primary children often has a snapshot quality, however unintentional, when they write "all about" pieces. Older and more sophisticated writers might take a closer look at this technique for their own writing; the snapshot strategy can be useful when writing an informal character sketch.

FLASHBACK

Tomorrow is Labor Day. The Fletcher Clan will gather, will eat, laugh, sing. But mostly we will reminisce, telling stories of the good old days. This tendency to be pulled into the past is deeply rooted in human nature. The flashback is a simple way for a writer to revisit the past in a piece of writing. Most flashbacks utilize a structure that is nearly circular. They begin in the present, go back to the past, return to the present, and then continue through the present.

A flashback can come at the very beginning of a book (*Flying Solo* or *Sarah, Plain and Tall*) or in the middle (*A Chair for My Mother*). It can encompass a very brief moment (*Hatchet*) or something quite long. In Jean Craighead George's novel *Julie of the Wolves,* the entire second section of the book is a flashback on Julie's unhappy and failed marriage.

A flashback can go a long way toward illuminating the present. The flashbacks in the story at the end of the previous chapter help explain the narrator's precarious emotional state.

The picture book shown on the following pages in Figure 11-1 was written by Tamiko and illustrated by Aisha, both sixth graders in New York City. It's interesting that while Tamiko's book deals with an unpleasant subject, divorce, her flashback recalls happier times. The difference between those good times and the divorce creates a satisfying tension in the book. For me, even more than the girl's reunion with her father, the flashback carries the highest emotional moment in the book. The close-up of the three ice-cream cones (the bigger the issue, the smaller you write) poignantly evokes a time when the family was intact.

OMISSION

When you write you don't have to include every single event that happened. You can leave stuff out. You *should* leave stuff out.

A young man nervously prepares for a first date. The writer begins this story by describing him carefully shaving, picking out a shirt—no, too fussy—and putting it back, finding another one, checking the clock, checking his wallet. He takes a deep breath and leaves his apartment. Is it necessary for the writer to describe this young man walking to the subway station, buying a ticket, waiting for the train? No.

> . . . He looked in the mirror one last time, took a deep breath, and stepped out of his apartment.

Figure 11-1

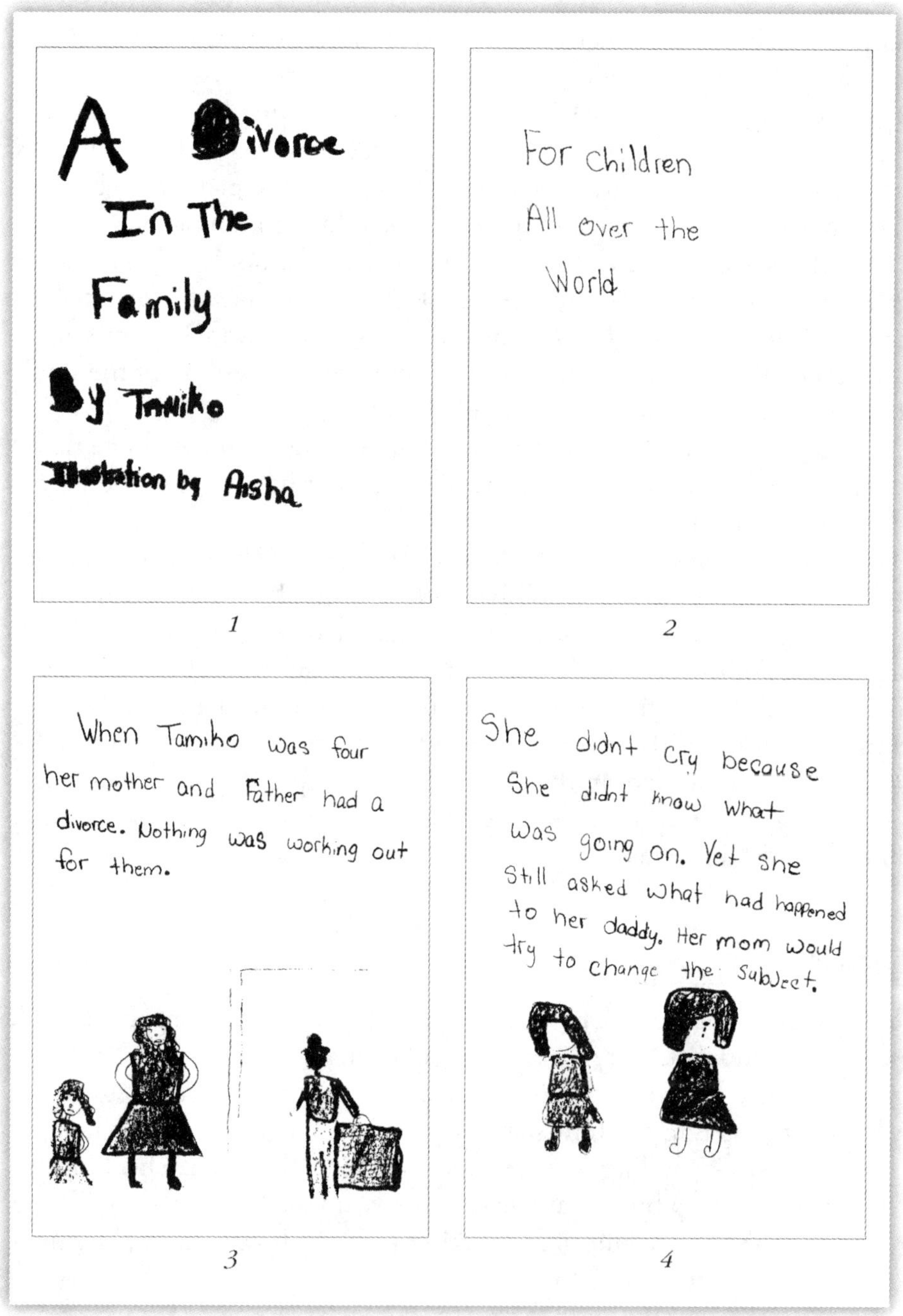

Panel 1:

A Divorce
In The
Family

By Tamiko

Illustration by Aisha

1

Panel 2:

For children
All over the
World

2

Panel 3:

When Tamiko was four
her mother and Father had a
divorce. Nothing was working out
for them.

3

Panel 4:

She didnt cry because
she didnt know what
was going on. Yet she
still asked what had happened
to her daddy. Her mom would
try to change the subject.

4

Figure 11-1 *(continued)*

Figure 11-1 *(continued)*

9

And when the icecream truck came daddy would buy three icecream cones.

Ice Cream

10

Chocolate for mommy, Butter Pecan for me and Strawberry for him.

Chocolate   ButterPecan   Strawberry

11

We had some of the best times together

12

as Tamiko grew up, She realized that her daddy was never coming back.

Figure 11-1 *(continued)*

He found her name in the long list beneath the row of mailboxes on the buzzer: C. Terranova. He pressed it, and the loud buzzer made him jump. The doorman eyed him suspiciously. . . .

A lengthy description of how he got to her apartment building, which train he took, etc., is unnecessary. The writer may *decide* to include it—to build suspense or to reveal a character's state of mind—but it can be omitted. The reader is fully capable of accounting for the time between leaving his apartment and buzzing her apartment. Such omissions are crucial if the writer is to grasp the next strategy.

FOCUS

We need to teach students how to write small, not just in terms of detail (the blue veins on the back of my grandmother's hands) but also in terms of moments, slices of time. In Dav Pilkey's *The Paperboy,* a boy delivers newspapers with the help of his dog. The entire story takes place in the early morning, before the rest of the household has woken up. "And this is the time when they are the happiest."

I'm leery of prewriting exercises, classrooms where each student is required to complete one before starting the writing. However, a simple map or time line may help students stand back from their experiences and gain a degree of detachment from the element of time in their writing, particularly when it comes to *focus.*

One summer day when I was about eleven and my family was on vacation, at the beach, I met another boy, Jonathan. We started palling around together the way kids do. We dug a huge seawall together to hold back the high tide. Within an hour, without talking all that much, we became quite close. It wasn't a hurried closeness (though we both knew we would likely never see each other after that afternoon), but in that short time we developed a sympathetic vision. I could see the world through his eyes, and it was a bright and glorious world. I think he saw something similar through my eyes. We ate lunch in a sand fort we had made. A few hours later we said goodbye. When he walked away I knew I was seeing the last of my best friend.

A time line of this experience might look something like this:

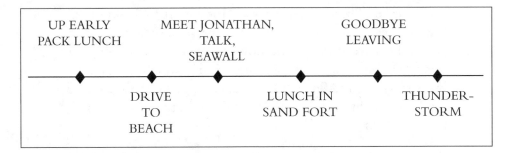

The crux of this day was the time spent with Jonathan. If I circle just that part of the time line and omit the rest, I might expand that part. Now I can begin to see the story taking shape in a new way.

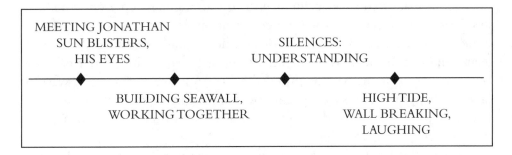

Focus does not mean writing shorter pieces. The crucial aspect of focus is that getting narrower allows the writer to go deeper, to get under the surface of a story by delving into one particular part of it.

Writing about a single, narrowed duration of time is only one kind of focus. A writer might also focus time by looking at repetitive events over time: habits, rituals, traditions. In Patricia Polacco's *The Keeping Quilt,* for example, we see how a quilt plays a central part in family traditions through several generations. We might think of this kind of time focus as vertical rather than horizontal.

SLOWING TIME

Young writers tend to give equal attention to each part of a story:

> We came to school but we were only there ten minutes before we got on the bus again! We took a ride. The bus stopped at MacDonald's and we had breakfast there. I couldn't eat all

> my pancakes. Then we got back on the bus. It took almost an
> hour to get to the zoo. There was a line so we had to wait to
> get in. First we went to the lions and tigers. I felt sorry for
> them. Next we went to the House of Primates. An orangutan
> bit Brendan on the finger. Our teacher flipped out. One of the
> mothers bought us ice cream. We had hamburgers for lunch. In
> the afternoon . . .

A third grader created this story. The writer is remarkably fair: he gives equal time to the breakfast stop at MacDonald's, the long line, Brendan's accident, etc. There is little sense that one event might be more important (and deserve more space, more words) than the others.

I sense that Brendan's accident with the orangutan represents the "hot spot" (or climax) in this story. A note of caution: As teachers we cannot presume to know exactly where the hot spot lies in students' stories. What may seem important to us may be of little interest to the writer, and vice versa. But once the student has identified the hot spot, we can suggest ways of slowing the writing. By slowing time, by lingering at the crucial moment, the writer helps the reader to discover the relative importance of various events and characters in the writing.

One of the most effective ways of slowing time is to write a dramatic scene. First, however, the writer must clearly understand the difference between a dramatic scene and a narrative summary.

> Last night my father came home and told us he'd been
> fired. We were all shocked. He stayed up til after midnight
> talking to my mother about it. When I went to bed I was so
> worried I couldn't sleep.

This narrative summary typifies much of the narrative prose written by students: controlled, distant, passive. In such writing, the narrator plants himself squarely between the reader and subject. All the story's raw material gets filtered through (and, in many cases, deadened by) the narrator. Here the reader has no evidence that "everyone was shocked" except that the narrator says so. In a dramatic scene, the narrator gives the reader a direct experience of sights, sounds, and events:

> When Dad walked in the door, his tie was open; his shoul-
> ders were slumped.

"Hiya, Dad," I said, but he didn't seem to hear. He put his briefcase on the kitchen table and looked through me.

"Your mother," he said at last. "I need to talk to your mother." He started walking toward the stairway.

Richard Price compares the difference between a dramatic scene and a narrative summary to the difference between being at a stadium for a baseball game and reading the box scores of the game in the newspaper. Real fans would always rather be at the game, hearing the crack of the bat, smelling the hot dogs. The dramatic scene is a powerful tool that can do many things:

- Slow the action
- Introduce dialogue and gesture
- Make the narrator an active character rather than a passive storyteller
- Allow the reader to experience the grief/delight of the story at the same time the narrator does
- Give readers the raw materials of the story so they can infer larger issues

In a movie, the director chooses carefully where to use slow motion to draw out a crucial scene. This technique usually comes at the film's hot spot—the farewell kiss, reunion, winning touchdown catch. A director would never film the entire movie in slow motion; the technique would quickly lose its novelty and become tedious. In the same way, a writer would not write a whole story in dramatic fashion—unless, perhaps, she was writing a play. A good narrative should have a *balance* of scene and summary. The writer thinks long and hard about which part is crucial enough to render as a dramatic scene.

Those of us who teach writing should become sensitized to how time is handled in texts. We can do this in our own reading and writing. Even with our help, young writers will have trouble with this element of writing. Time is tricky—professional writers have a great deal of difficulty with it. Writing teachers need to be alive to the tiniest breakthroughs their students make—even accidental ones—toward a more fluid, playful sense of time in their writing.

The story in Figure 11-2 on the following pages was written by a kindergarten child in Queens, New York. As you read it, and enjoy the intimate voice, notice also how well this young writer plays with time: first building suspense, then lingering on a particular moment, then jumping into the future.

Figure 11-2

1. My baby is a cry baby and is so cute. I love him so much. His name is Tal.

2. Tomorrow he will come home and I will help my mother. We will get him to sleep. I saw him three times.

3. I am ready for him. His carriage is ready. I will pull him in his carriage slowly...

4. ...slowly now, he is home. He likes to cry and sleep. Shhhhhhhhhh...

Figure 11-2 *(continued)*

5. *Shhhhhhhhh When he is sleeping I play because he cries so much. And I help my mother.*

6. *And when he sleeps he is cute, very cute. And when he sleeps he is quiet.*

7. *I help my mother. And when my mother nurses him I play.*

8. *Now he is six months. He was born March 7.*

Twelve

UNFORGETTABLE LANGUAGE

*The bags under his eyes were pouches containing the
smuggled memories of a disappointing life.*

—GRAHAM GREENE, *A Burnt-Out Case*

WHEN I WAS a senior in high school, my mother had a baby: Carolyn. While it was great being that old and having a new baby sister, I found it plenty tough to leave her when I went off to college. I sorely missed Carolyn and tried hard to stay in touch. When she was two, I shaved off my first failed beard, stuffed those whiskers into an envelope, and mailed that beard to her. I have always had a special relationship with Carolyn; I'm her oldest brother and, as I'm fond of reminding her, her godfather.

When I came home from college Carolyn would be eager to play with me. I was happy to do so, though I also had other fish to fry: work, sports, movies, sometimes even the occasional date. One day, when Carolyn was four, I tried to explain it to her.

"Look, I can't play now. I'm really busy today. How about tomorrow?" She flounced away and looked back at me, frowning hard.

"The minute you come home," she snapped, "you put on the cloak of busyness!"

This book would not be complete without a chapter that at least touches on beautiful writing, truly original language, images that make you sit up straight when you're reading.

In *The Relatives Came,* Cynthia Rylant describes how the house felt different at night with relatives sleeping all over the place: "It was different with all that new breathing in the house."

A sentence like this makes me start talking to myself, repeating it over and over. A sentence like this made me want to be a writer in the first place.

Writers have particular writers they go to for inspiration. They read the words of the masters over and over, awed, forever relearning the trade (how does she *do* that anyway?), thrilling to the power and beauty of language in the hands of a gifted writer. Such "writerly writers" represent a select club. Thomas Mann, Virginia Woolf. For Raymond Carver: Anton Chekhov. For Cynthia Rylant: James Agee and William Maxwell. For me: Vladimir Nabokov, Annie Dillard, and Richard Ford. Also Martin Amis, who seems incapable of writing a stale sentence. His prose crackles with originality: "You can kill time in a number of ways but it always depends on the kind of time you're fighting: some time is unkillable, immortal" (from *Money*).

I keep an eye out for killer sentences like that, or like the lovely one I found in *Atticus*, a novel by Ron Hansen: "Weed and sage were yellow against the snow and the snow strayed over the geography as though recalling how it was to be water." (p. 3)

Or from Steinbeck's *East of Eden:* "There would be five or six wet and wonderful years when there might be nineteen to twenty-five inches of rain, and the land would shout with grass." (p. 5) An arresting image: I would have never thought to describe it in such a way—that the land could *shout* with grass.

But you don't necessarily have to go to published books to find original language. I often take inspiration from very young children. Some children seem to speak a kind of unschooled poetry, however unintentional or inaccurate. Hearing them, I understand why Romantic poets like William Wordsworth believed that "the child is father to the man."

Words come alive in the mouth of my stepson Adam. I am startled by what he says as much as by the way he says it. For the past few years I have used my journal to record his best one-liners, his pithiest aphorisms.

Adam, four years old. I give him a huge yellow leaf I found in the woods. "Look," he exclaims. "A primary color!"

Adam at five. He loves the bath but hates getting out of the tub. He stands there, shivering. "Quick, Ralphie, wrap me up!" he cries. "I'm soaking cold!"

Adam coming down for breakfast: "When I woke up my eyes were like two eggs cracking open."

Listening to music, Adam points at the radio: "I want to be *in* there, right in there with that music."

Adam eating pizza topped with black olives: "Hey, there's a blizzard of olives under here!"

I ask Adam to clean his room. But when I get upstairs the room looks messy.

"What are you doing?" I ask, giving him a suspicious look. Across the room, he squirms and laughs.

"Stop it, you're tickling me with your voice!"

When JoAnn was pregnant, it dawned on Adam that he would no longer be the youngest child. You could see him trying to figure out his new place in the family. One day JoAnn and I talked about throwing away some junk in our attic. Adam listened closely.

"Would you ever throw *me* away?" he asked, dead serious.

"Absolutely not," JoAnn assured him. "We love you much too much for that."

"That's a rule," Adam said seriously, lifting his index finger for emphasis. "No throwing people away."

I have watched Adam trying to figure out my role as stepfather. Usually he is the first one to wake up, but one morning I have to go into his room to rouse him. I rub his back, singing softly: "You are my sunshine, my only sunshine." He gives me a tender, frowning look.

"I'm not your sunshine," he says softly. "I'm your son."

When Adam was four years old my mother took him for a walk.

"Take my hand," she said. "We're crossing the street."

"I know, Grandma," Adam said. "You *are* getting old."

As a writer, I admire Adam's language tremendously. I admire his fearlessness, his expansive playfulness, the fluidity with which he puts images together. Who would think of putting "blizzard" next to "pizza"? An odd image but it works. Maybe all images that sound new are essentially odd. The expression "soaking cold" is not commonplace, yet we all know exactly what he means.

The spoken language of young children makes me think of molten lava: steaming, flowing, magnificent. Their written language can be that way, too, with images that take our breath away and allow us to see the tired old world with new eyes.

"Smoking is like eating fire." John (third grade)

"The wind makes raindrops curve when they fall. When they fall on the ground they self-destruct." Lauren (second grade)

"The sky holds the earth in its arms." Ramona (third grade)

The moon
A monster's eye,
The stars
His shiny teeth . . . Jenny (second grade)

I have noticed that when children learn the proper conventions, often their language cools to safe "correctness." When you look at the writing of older children, you're less likely to find the same degree of freedom, the bold images and striking metaphors that you see with younger children. Why? It may have something to do with the expectations adults have for children and their language use as they mature in school.

"In school we don't value experimentation as much as correctness," notes JoAnn Portalupi. "We've broken out of that box a little bit with skills, inventive spelling, but not yet with language. We don't look for the surprise in language—we look for language that gets the job done."

We start creating an environment that encourages original language by *expecting* mistakes. When I work with children, I keep a sharp lookout for those words, phrases, and sentences that are "wrong but wonderful":

"I'm sorry, Adam, but I can't seem to put this toy together," JoAnn says.

"But Mom," Adam protests, "it explains it right in the destructions!"

Most of us would smile at such an error. We appreciate Adam's courageous attempt at pronouncing such a big word, how "destructions" is also a three-syllable word that rhymes with "instructions," the way his mispronunciation touches on another kind of truth about children's toys. We are not worried that Adam's sentence is not "right" because we know that it is on the way to being right. In the meantime, the humorous error strikes me as more interesting than the right word.

"Will you please behave?" an exasperated mother tells her son.

"*I am* being *have!*" the boy retorts.

Garp's son feared the "under-toad" (undertow) in *The World According to Garp* by John Irving. The same boy used to tell people that his mother was going to "gradual school." My stepson Taylor used to ask me about the "World Serious" when he was five.

Figure 12-1

Daniel   Dec: 61,- 1987.

Shdossoszi   in The diro

Shatossoszi   in The diro

Swaofinllin   all   ova   my

wll   on to   my   llap

like, a   hoss   jimpbin.

Shadows in the air
Shadows in the air
Swiffeling all over my wall
Onto my lap
Like a horse jumping

Figure 12-2

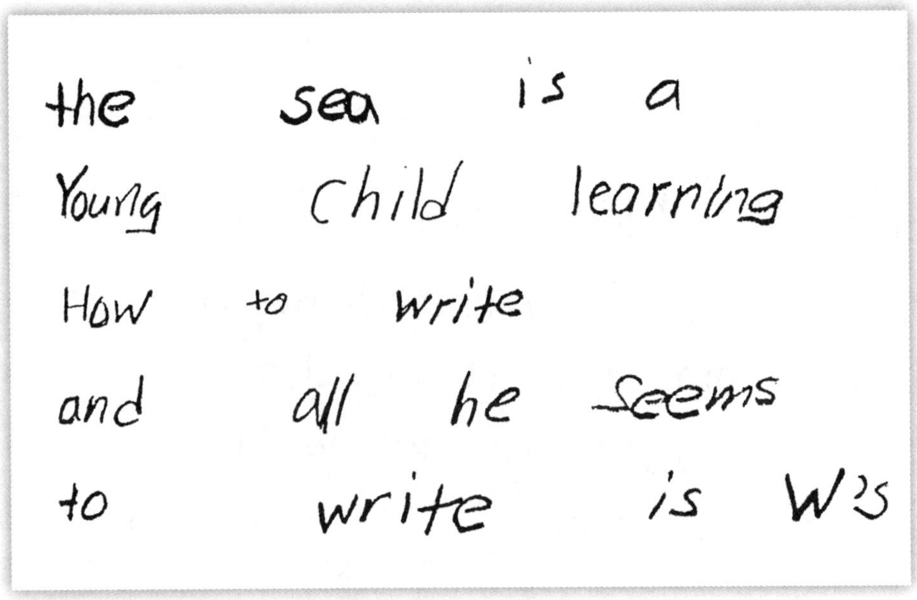

the   sea   is   a
Young   child   learning
How   to   write
and   all   he   ~~Seems~~
to   write   is   W²s

In Figure 12-1 on the previous page, the poem by Daniel, a first grader at PS 178, the Bronx, has one word that is "wrong but wonderful":

"Swiffeling" is not a word, though it seems to me that it *should* be a word. In fact, it sounds like the perfect word for the peculiar way shadows move across a wall. Writers have been known to make up a word where none exists. In *The Ghost-Eye Tree,* Bill Martin and John Archambault concocted the word "foolie" to describe those scary thoughts that bedevil your mind when you're walking in the dark.

If you're looking for place to find striking language, poetry is a good place to start. Seven-year-old Andrew Park, a student in Lisa Lenz's class in Caldwell, New Jersey, read Langston Hughes' poem "Long Trip." The poem moved Andrew to write a poem about the sea (see Figure 12-2 above).

In the poem shown in Figure 12-3, Vanessa Hawkins, a second grader in Sea Cliff, New York, takes on the persona of a star. Her poem challenges the old song that advises you to "catch a falling star and put it in your pocket."

It's true that certain kids seem to have a knack for poetic expression, but I strongly believe that original writing can be taught, or at least fostered. Writing teachers can do several things to help children revitalize the language in their writing. First, we need to attune the ears of young writers to magical language wherever they hear it—in books, poems, the writing of their peers,

Figure 12-3

Stars
we twinkle in the
cold sky air we are there
all night if you try to
pull us down we will
burn a hole in your pocket
by Vanessa Hawkins.

dialogue. One fourth-grade student remembered this snatch of conversation with her father one morning and used it to start her story:

> "C'mon," her father said. He shook her. "UP!"
> "What time is it?" she mumbled, staring out the dark window.
> "It's o-dark-thirty," he said crisply. "Time to rise!"

We must also beware the acronyms and curriculum clichés that creep into our classroom—test prep, ESL, G & T—those shortcut labels that help us to categorize at the expense of exploring ideas in depth. We need to find new ways to say old things—and this takes work. For example, in this chapter I deliberately avoided using the words "fresh language," a phrase used so often it has lost the newness it must have once had.

Here is one strategy for writing in an original fashion: *write what you see, not what you are supposed to see.* Art students learn the same thing. The brain takes the discordant images of the world and organizes them into the coherent and familiar things of our worlds: house, moon, bus, comb. A writer learns the fresh power that results from presenting raw images *before* they have been reorganized and homogenized:

"My father's head was floating in the hot tub."
"The moon was tangled in the oak tree's branches."
"A dark tarantula of keys lay on the kitchen counter."

We know, of course, that the moon is more than a quarter million miles from earth; still, it *looks* like it gets caught in the branches of the tree. That might be an original way of saying it. I knew that the entire body of my father was floating in the hot tub, but I could only see his head. This unreconstructed image makes the sentence come alive in a new, if disturbing, way.

As writing teachers we should highlight those moments when students create powerful images, when they use language to boldly extend their thinking. For instance, Thomas wrote a story that begins:

Many, many years ago, in the Southwestern United States, there was a very beautiful forest. It was so beautiful and famous for its splendor that before you entered it you had to genuflect. . . .

The use of "genuflect" is surprising. It represents a bold and original attempt to communicate the sense of awe and reverence he felt upon entering this forest.

Startling language can give the reader a dazzling jolt of recognition (literally: to re-think), as in the poem by Erin Spampinato (see Figure 12-4), a six-year-old in Lisa Lenz's first-grade classroom in Caldwell, New Jersey. One day Erin was idly watching her best friend lying on the rug, reading. The girl had a braid that hung down onto the book. Suddenly it looked to Erin as if the braid were an actual link between brain and book. This image inspired Erin's poem "Meghan"; I don't know if I have read a better one about reading.

Figure 12-4

Her braid hangs dangling and creeps down her mind into the page.

Thirteen

WRITING NONFICTION

Don't get too close. Astronomers are reporting that they have taken the measure of the biggest, baddest black holes yet found in the universe, abyssal yawns 10 times the size of our solar system into which billions of Suns have vanished like a guilty thought.

—*"Astronomers Find Biggest Black Holes Yet" by Dennis Overbye*, New York Times, Dec. 5, 2011

I ONCE TOOK a writing course from novelist Gail Godwin. In a soft North Carolina drawl, she spoke to us about how each writer must find the right idea to write about.

"Too often a writer picks an idea that turns out to be nothing more than a *solander*," she said.

We looked at her blankly. Solander?

"A solander is a book-object," she explained. "Tell me if this has ever happened to you. You're at a party at someone's house, and you choose a book from a bookcase. But when you take it down and try to open it up, there aren't any pages. In fact you realize it's not a book at all. Instead, you find some object inside—a cigarette lighter. A silver flask."

We nodded. Certainly, we had seen them. And it gave a certain satisfaction to learn that *solander* was the precise noun for these imposters. But what did that have to do with choosing a good idea to write about?

Godwin anticipated this question by reading aloud from *Technique in Fiction,* by Robie Macauley and George Lanning:

"Learning to write sometimes seems like a succession of waste motions, and among the most wasteful is that one which urges us to commit to paper a fiction which—though it may look solid enough, though it may even be bought for publication—is as hollow, as much a trick, as those boxes which people make by cutting out the center of a book and gluing together the edges of the pages. These are called solanders, and few are the writers who have not perpetrated a fair number of solander-fictions in their time."

This makes a valid point about fiction, but it applies to nonfiction as well. Nonfiction readers bring a number of expectations when they sit down to read. The first one is intelligent insight. Before style or technique, we are drawn to writing that challenges our intellect. We demand pages and paragraphs and sentences that make us think. Readers are selfish: We insist on being enriched by whatever we read. We want to go somewhere we've never gone before.

This cannot be stated bluntly enough: The writer must have something to say.

It may seem strange to find such an important chapter near the end of this book. The truth is that all the preceding chapters are meaningless unless the writer can find something interesting and important to say about the subject. It doesn't matter if a writer begins it cleverly or ends it neatly, organizes it smoothly, writes it dramatically, writes it with voice. The "it" itself has to have merit. This holds true for all genres, but particularly for nonfiction.

In a first-grade class I watched a young teacher pass around some paper.

"I want you to think of any important ideas you might write about," she tells the kids. "You can write those important ideas down on the paper."

She hands a piece of paper to Michael, the strongest writer in the class, but today he frowns up at her.

"I'll need a couple sheets," he says. "You know my letters are still pretty big. I can't write too small."

"That's okay," she says. "You can have all the paper you want."

But instead of writing, Michael just sits there.

"What's wrong?" she asks, kneeling beside him.

"See, I'm not sure I understand what you want us to do," he says. "Do you want us to write ideas that are important—or ideas that are *significant*?"

Michael's precocious question, the distinction between important and significant, seems worth exploring in the context of nonfiction. When you think about it, there's little inherently interesting about most subjects. Depending on how it is handled, a subject can seem lively or it can put us to sleep. The sole difference lies in what the writer brings to the subject at hand. Our best nonfiction writers find significance in subjects that might seem terminally boring. David Owen, a staff writer for *The New Yorker*, can make mundane topics (Barbie dolls, the history of photocopiers) positively sing when he writes about them. So can Rick Bragg.

OLYMPICS: SKELETON; Skeleton Plunges Face-First Back Into the Winter Games

By Rick Bragg (*New York Times*, February 18, 2002)

SALT LAKE CITY, Feb. 17—Picture riding the lid of a turkey roaster pan down a roller coaster rail after an ice storm.

Picture it at almost 80 miles an hour, with wicked turns, at G-forces so powerful that you cannot raise your helmet from the ice, which glitters just an inch away.

Now picture making that ride face first.

"I was screaming inside my helmet," said Chris Soule, as he described the first time he tried the ominous-sounding sport of skeleton. It returns to these Olympic Winter Games after a 54-year ban.

Soule, the 2002 World Cup gold medalist from Trumbull, Conn., says it is not as dangerous as it looks, sliding down a twisting, turning course belly down on a tiny sled, his helmeted head leading the way.

That may be, but whenever he tells the Olympic athletes in other sports what he is there for, they say much the same thing: "Oh. You guys are crazy."

Perhaps it is appropriate that international competitions for this event, perhaps the most perilous of all here, now begin with a moment of silence.

There is no affectation here, no baggy pants and thrash music like the snowboarders have, no ice skater's sequins and storied history, no cinematic skiing glory, acted out by a rugged Robert Redford, as in the downhill.

This is just fast and mean and a little bit insane, and if you mess up, if you are clumsy and brush the wall, there is pain and often blood. Soule used to wrap parts of his body in duct tape—the ice on the walls tended to eat his sweater off his arm.

Now, after petitioning Olympic officials to reinstate the sport—which gets its name because frames of earlier sleds resembled a skeleton—he and the rest of the world's most daring sliders will get a running start, hurl themselves and their sleds down a chute of hard ice and show the world what it means to ride the bones. The men's and women's competitions are scheduled for Wednesday.

"I haven't told my mother yet," said Lincoln DeWitt, one of Soule's Olympic teammates, when asked what his family thought of his competition here, which has been banned not once but twice from the Games.

It is a sport ruled, and abused, by gravity.

Bragg won a Pulitzer Prize for feature writing in 1996, and here you can see why. This is a virtuoso piece of nonfiction writing. It has an arresting lead, strategic quotes, precise details, vivid description, plus a striking use of verbs (my favorite sentence is the one where "the ice . . . tended to eat the sweater off his arm"). Bragg takes an obscure Olympic sport and transforms it into an article you cannot put down.

LIFE AS A FREELANCE WRITER

I spent fifteen years working as a freelance writer, mostly writing feature articles and essays. Since then I have written many how-to books for students about writing. Over time, I have learned which subjects have real potential and which do not. When I write nonfiction, I look for a subject with two distinguishing characteristics: It must interest me, and it must be something about which I've got something to say.

It has been said that the trick to being a successful freelance writer is to specialize in one particular subject: music, medical breakthroughs, the parent-child relationship, etc. Specializing saves time: You don't have to take a crash course on a new subject every time you write a new article. Alas, I have not specialized. Instead I have written and published articles on a wide range of subjects including Al Oerter (Olympic gold medal winner in the discus), bartering, buying a franchise, computer screen glare, the Museum of Natural History, lithographer Tatyana Grosman, the Animal Medical Center in Manhattan, Harrods of London, a quadriplegic doctor.

In each case, my original fascination with the subject had seeds in my own life. Both Tatyana Grosman and Al Oerter were residents of West Islip, New York, where my family lived for twenty years. I often watched Oerter, benevolent giant, pass our house on his morning runs. I made frequent visits to Harrods while I was taking corporate tours to London.

One day at the beach I noticed that the wife of a close friend had a rose tattooed on her leg just above the ankle. I asked her about it; the question unleashed a long passionate reply about her tattoo. I had never before been interested in tattoos. But listening to her story, I found myself leaning forward. (This was well before tattoos had become fashionable.) This conversation led directly to an article I wrote for *Cosmopolitan* about professional women who get a tattoo on their bodies.

Too many students write on issues or subjects they know nothing about. While professional writers—and some amateurs—can make themselves care about almost any subject through sheer will, this feat lies beyond the reach of most writers. If we sense that students are writing about topics they don't know or care about, we might suggest they choose another idea, something closer to the heart. My best subjects seem to be those that anger, appall, baffle, or exasperate me. I look for a subject with *resonance:* that internal echo you hear when you thump it. Students who find themselves writing dispirited prose should look harder at themselves and ask: Where do *I* stand on this? What's *my* point of view? Forget what the experts say: What part amazes or angers *me?*

On the other hand, I don't necessarily look for a subject about which I am already an expert. Total expertise can be as dangerous as total ignorance. Inside experts with *too* much knowledge of a subject typically produce the worst writing in many technical subjects (manuals for cameras, computers, or insurance). Such writing is notoriously opaque, voiceless, and filled with jargon.

A healthy dose of ignorance is often helpful when you begin researching a subject: It keeps you honest; it keeps you humble. It insures that you will be a learner. It gives you room to expand into the majesty or the heartbreak of whatever subject you are writing about. It provides room for the imagination, which, as the writer Bruce Brooks has pointed out, flows from what is known to what is not known.

I value my ignorance when I write nonfiction. I start with this axiom: In most ways I am like everyone else. The questions I have are the same questions my reader will have. I figure if I can make something understandable and interesting to myself, I can make it understandable and interesting to my readers.

Often I'm not one hundred percent sure I can write well about a subject, but if I'm sufficiently intrigued I'll give it a try. *Boy Writers: Reclaiming Their Voices* began with a nagging question—why are so many boys struggling in writing classrooms? I lived this question for a solid year. Once again, I found it helpful to write from abundance. I took a crash course on the subject. I read a dozen books on gender studies and interviewed hundreds of boys and teachers, before I could finally sit down to write the book.

FACTUAL INSIGHT

Insight may be communicated through the facts a writer digs up. Nonfiction writers fill notebooks with odd facts, tidbits, statistics, and tuck these factual nuggets, raisin-like, into the loaves of their writing. For instance, at the time of Robert's birth, my journal contained these facts that I will use one day in some piece of writing:

- Many babies are born leaking milk from their own breasts. This is sometimes known as "witch's milk."
- Rarely, a baby is born with the amniotic sac still intact. This is known as being born "in the caul."
- An infant's suck is five to ten times as strong as the suck of an adult.
- Studies show that a baby can see light from within the womb.
- During the birth process, two separate bodily systems ensure that the baby's brain continues to get an uninterrupted supply of oxygen.
- After birth, in some Polynesian cultures, the placenta is placed in the earth along with a tree sapling. After nourishing the fetus, the placenta nourishes the baby tree.

These facts are not invented or imagined; they are drawn directly from the actual world. In one sense, the nonfiction writer acts as a teller-of-secrets. During my research I try to dig up lots of facts, though I know I won't necessarily use them all in any article. Rather, I'll select the best facts from among them. Donald Murray explained that skilled nonfiction writers work from abundance: "It takes thirty gallons of sap to make a gallon of maple syrup; it takes hundreds of pages of notes to make one *Reader's Digest* article."

Diane Ackerman's wonderful book *A Natural History of the Senses* is replete with provocative facts:

- The average body has about five million hairs.
- Massaged (premature) babies gain weight as much as fifty percent faster than unmassaged babies.
- "In Japan, chefs offer the flesh of the puffer fish, or *fugu,* which is highly poisonous unless prepared with exquisite care. The most distinguished chefs leave just enough of the poison in the flesh to make the diners' lips tingle, so they know how close they are coming to their mortality."

In an unpublished short story of mine, "Friday Night at the Spider Fights," I had enormous fun writing one passage filled with delicious facts I had collected about spiders:

> Coop knew spiders the way dentists know bad breath—I mean he *knew* them, inside and out. He taught me that there are 30,000 spider species in the world. The 650 species in New York and New England alone equal the number of bird species breeding in all of North America, north of Mexico. The biggest spider in the world is the "bird-eating spider" (*Theraphosa*) of South America. They found one with a body three inches long with a ten-inch leg span fully extended. That's a lot of spidermeat for a starving man. The smallest spider in the world is the *Patu marplesi* of Western Samoa, found in moss at an altitude of 2,000 feet. It measures about half the size of a printed period (.) The fastest spider in the world is *Tegenaria atrica*. This spider has been clocked at 1.73 feet per second, or 1.17 mph. That may not sound fast, but it is a speed of 33 times its body length per second, compared to the human record of $5\frac{1}{3}$ times its body length per second. Our spider, Antaeus III, was a *Tegenaria domestica,* close relative of the fleet *Tegenaria atrica.* . . ."

Years later this paragraph would become the seed for my middle grade novel, *Spider Boy.* In the book the main character keeps a journal containing similar facts about spiders; selections of his journal are included in the story. It's a work of fiction, but I had to read nine nonfiction books in order to write it. One fifth-grader wrote me a letter in which he said: "*Spider Boy* taught me a ton about spiders. It's more a book of <u>faction</u> than fiction."

Facts can be illuminating, but facts by themselves won't carry the day. Too much dense information can sink a piece of nonfiction writing. Facts must be interspersed with narrative or anecdote, the information humanized through voice, humor, and wit. Consider this piece of writing by Blake, an eighth grader from New York:

THE FIRST DEAD PERFORMANCE

When I recently visited the Tower of London in England, I heard a very interesting story from a tour guide at the site where stood the scaffold on which two of Henry VIII's wives were executed, Anne Boleyn and Catherine Howard.

To understand this story one must know that there was an entire ceremony to having one's head chopped off. First, you would stand on your scaffold and give a speech, thanking your relatives for being there, and explaining what should be done about your body and possessions. While the above ritual would be of dubious importance today, it was considered in poor taste and altogether dishonorable if one insisted on being carried kicking and screaming to the axeman. Following that, you would tip the executioner. In fact, this is where the word "tip" comes from today. It stands for the words "to insure promptness." The higher the tip, the faster, and less drawn out, would be your end.

One day the Duchess of Salisbury was scheduled to be executed. After her speech, she tipped the executioner a sterling silver tea set. This was the equivalent of a year's worth of salary for an executioner. As the Duchess knelt down by the block, everything seemed just dandy, for such a macabre setting. However, unbeknownst to everyone present, the executioner was only an apprentice, and this was his first live execution.

At the grim moment we can imagine the nervous young axeman winding up, perhaps his tongue hanging out in concentration. Suddenly, he brought his axe down in a shining, whirling arc . . . and missed. He actually hit the lady's shoulder. Hell hath no fury as one who receives less than his or her money's worth, especially in this instance. The old woman leaped up and began a long catalogue of personal remarks about the executioner's family. While she was in this state, the axeman took an unexpected swing at her. She ducked. Then she panicked. She began running around the scaffold like a chicken deprived of its head with the axeman swinging his axe to and fro, running behind her. He missed her a total of seven times before her head finally came off.

Although you may think this a morbid example of humor, it is a very good idea of what the old English thought to be funny. It does generate a certain amusement and, besides, keep a stiff upper lip, as the English might say.

This nonfiction piece is written with a lively voice that makes it a pleasure to read. But it's more than just a great story; it also contains a number of what detectives call "hard facts." The reader feels enriched to learn the origin of the word "tip," for example. Without this historically accurate information Blake's piece wouldn't be nearly as effective.

INTERPRETIVE INSIGHT

In the end, nonfiction readers expect more from the writer than juicy trivia or factual accuracy. They expect the nonfiction writer to *interpret* this factual information. Vivid metaphors are a great tool for doing that. Here's how writer Bob Shacochis describes the origin of a hurricane:

Now, if a vortex deepened at the center of the storm and if the clouds walled up into an eye, forming a chimney for evaporating water to be sucked heavenward off the ocean—if these things happened, we'd have a hurricane: a massive, self-sustaining heat engine, siphoning excess warmth out of the ocean and taking it on a parabolic ride west and north, its intention to balance the earth's heat budget, spreading around the surplus at cooler latitudes.

Great sentence! Shacochis takes facts that are available to any writer and finds bold metaphors ("self-sustaining heat engine . . . on a parabolic ride . . . to balance the earth's heat budget") that help us to see these facts in a new light.

The following essay, written by another eighth grader, has an edgy tone that carries a satisfying bite. Like other examples of successful nonfiction writing, this essay has much to commend it: voice, dark humor, and language play. But more than anything else I am swept along by the ideas and insight, the sheer unsentimental intelligence of this essay. Honestly, reading this essay changed the way I view my relationship with my children, and my relationship with my parents.

PARENTS

In all the animal kingdom, it is difficult to find a creature more proud, powerful, and predictably provocative than the Parent. Displaying a concern for their young that borders on the bothersome, members of this species have been observed exhibiting the following behaviors toward their offspring: they warn, threaten, order, judge, criticize, preach, advise, and lecture.

"Either that room gets cleaned up now, or else!"

"Can't you do anything right?"

"If I were you . . ."

"When I was your age . . ."

"You'll do as you're told."

Parents put you down, stereotype, humiliate, prophesize, nag, accuse, and name-call.

"You're acting like a baby."

"How can you be so stupid?"

"Don't you think of anyone except yourself?"

They also shame, coerce, trivialize, dash hopes, and interrogate.

"Why don't you act your age?"

"If you know what's good for you . . ."

"You're too young . . ."

They say one thing and do another. They tell you why you can't instead of how you might, what's wrong instead of what's right. It's all done in the name of love.

Some of you may think I'm being a little hard on parents. Look, I don't have anything against parents, not really. I know that there have been sightings of parents engaged in harmonious habitation with their children.

It's a funny thing in families: often, the greater the love and commitment between parents and children, the greater the conflict, the greater the hurt. It's precisely *because* people care, *because* they want to protect and guide and make over those they love in their own image, that so many problems develop. You want their love, respect, and approval, and they want yours. You have an investment in each other that you don't want to lose. It's the caring that makes you fight, and the fighting that makes you no longer care.

Now, let's get back to those bizarre birds who keep you under their wings, your parents. You remember them, the creatures with eyes in the back of their heads, and the ability to read minds. They're the ones who, out of genuine love and concern for your well-being, can do some damage. You've got to understand how they see you, how they see themselves, and how they see their role as parents.

Naturally, your parents want you to be happy, healthy, brilliant, responsible, athletic, neat, successful, honest, and well-mannered.

"Is that all?" you ask. No, not if your parents pressure you to excel. Then this modest set of expectations can only expand. All A's isn't good enough: if you're that smart, how about working harder to become valedictorian? Athletic? Well, let's see some leadership! Team captain, no less. College-bound? Could it mean anything that your mom grew ivy on the bars of your crib?

Parents can become so focused on what they want their kid to become that they lose sight of *who* their kid is. Should you be so lucky (?) to reach one of their goals, well, that's what they expect from you, your success is taken for granted and whoosh, before you can say Harvard Law School, they've swooped in with their sights on a new target.

Unfortunately, many parents judge their success as parents by the extent to which they can identify and correct "flaws" in their kids. What happens, sadly, is the destruction of the parent-child relationship. Instead of a loving, caring relationship between two *equals* (equals as human beings even if one has more experience or power than the other), you end up with a relationship based upon *roles* where the parent is dominant and the child is inferior. Once those roles are established, you can lose your identity.

It's as if you become an object instead of a person, a lump of clay that is molded. Somehow, in this Child Role you're made to feel less than equal, less than human, like a doll to be dressed and groomed in someone else's image. You lose your rights, you lose touch with your feelings, you become suspended between your parents' expectations and your true self. You become a mirror, a dream, an extension. You become property, "my kid," something to be owned. You become everything, everything except yourself.

Your parents, who seemingly have all the power, money and independence, can also feel rejected, unloved, and unappreciated. They see themselves as the people who have done more for you than anyone. They got up in the middle of the night to feed you, they sacrificed many of their plans and purchases for your benefit, and they know how important you are to their lives. This makes them feel entitled to your obedience and appreciation. When they don't get it, they feel resentful and hurt. They feel like they can't do anything right in your eyes; you've written them off as out of touch, narrow-minded, materialistic, overly concerned with what people think. You don't want to be seen with them, you don't like how they drive, what they wear, what they value.

And because of the cycle of criticism already established in the household, you lose no opportunity to peddle your disdain in their direction.

They feel ignored, misunderstood, and abused. They feel they're taken for granted, that they are seen as objects: a hander-out of money, a cooker, a cleaner, a chauffeur, a protector, a tutor. They feel stereotyped into the Parent Role, and in that role they feel that *they* are less than equal. They feel that their children don't care about them, and don't extend them courtesies that mere strangers would receive.

So just remember that they were kids just like us once. One day we'll be in *their* place.

Fourteen

REVISION

I'm not a very good writer,
but I'm an excellent rewriter.

—JAMES MICHENER

IN A SECOND-GRADE CLASS I met a girl named Rachita. She had a knack of creating wonderfully descriptive images when she spoke. Unfortunately they never made it into her writing. One day during a writing workshop she wrote a poem:

Bread and Jam

I love bread and jam.
I love it on Mondays, Tuesdays,
Wednesdays, Thursdays, Fridays....
I just looooooooooooooooooooooove
bread and jam!

"Well, I can tell that you really love bread and jam," I began.

"I sure do!" Her eyes sparkled. "This morning I put so much jam on my bread that when I took a bite I had a jam mustache!"

I laughed. "A jam mustache! Do you think you might want to add that to your poem?"

She shook her head. "Uh uh. I'm doing a new poem."

Rachita's teacher, who observed this conference, silently mouthed to me one word: *Stubborn!*

The next day I had another writing conference with Rachita. She had written a poem about a dog that had died.

My dog is dead,
oh no, oh no.
He got hit by a car.
I don't know what to do.

"That's all I've got so far," Rachita said glumly. "I'm kind've stuck."

I touched her on the arm. "I'm really sorry that your dog died. That's so sad!"

"I know." Solemnly she nodded. "We have a sandbox in my back yard, and even though my dog is dead you can still see her footprints in the sand. Her footprints are still there."

"Wow." I slowly shook my head. "That's such a powerful image. I can really picture that. Do you think . . . you might want to include that in your poem?"

"Nope." Suddenly she grinned. "Because guess what? I'm getting a new dog!"

Every writer needs to know how to revise. It's a crucial part of the skill set. E. B. White did nine drafts of *Charlotte's Web*. I began writing *The One O'Clock Chop* in 2003. Seven revisions later, in 2006, I finally finished the book. When I work with young writers I try to find accessible quotes to explain revision.

"In baseball you get three strikes and you're out," says Tomie dePaola. "In writing, you get as many whacks at the ball as you want until you finally get a hit."

Nevertheless, kids famously resist our encouragement to revise their writing. They groan when we urge them to go back, reread, and find ways to make the piece better. This anti-revision attitude can be frustrating to writing teachers, but I'm sympathetic because I have often felt it myself.

My first published book was *I Am Wings: Poems About Love*. My editor told me that she loved the book, which wouldn't even need any revision. It felt too good to be true; they were buying the book *as is*. One day the phone rang.

"There's just one image in a poem that doesn't quite work," my editor said. She referred me to the following poem:

Won't You Come Home Bill Bailey?

You liked vegetarian food
plus those old-time songs
that drove me up a wall

THE RAIN IN SPAIN

FALLS MAINLY ON THE PLAIN

I liked red meat (rare)
and rock music (hard)
I adored horror films
you loved books
and in a couple of months
we split up

I gave back your books
you gave back my CDs
and that seemed to end it
except for one thing

> *I AIN'T HAD NO LOVING SINCE*
> *JANUARY FEBRUARY JUNE AND JULY*

your old-fashioned songs
jumbling around in my head
like sneakers in a dryer
keeping me up day and night

> *REMEMBER THAT RAINY EVENING*
> *I THREW YOU OUT*
> *WITH NOTHING BUT A*
> *FINE-TOOTH COMB?*

Please come over right away
you gotta clean out this stuff

> *PLEASE RELEASE ME LET ME GO*
> *I DON'T LOVE YOU ANYMORE*

I mean it: I'm going nuts.

"That line about sneakers in a dryer doesn't work," my editor said. "You can't put sneakers in a dryer or they'll melt, right?

"Well, uh . . ." I stammered.

"I suggest we change that line to '*like sneakers in a washer,*'" the editor said. "What do you think?"

Leave it the way I wrote it, I thought, though I didn't say so. At that moment I was keenly aware of the power imbalance between Mighty Editor and struggling writer. *I Am Wings* would be my first published book for young readers. I envisioned that editor as a sentinel standing at the Gates Of Literature, and I was determined to walk through those gates. I didn't want to make any waves, so I reluctantly agreed to replace '*dryer*' with '*washer.*' No big deal, I told myself. People will hardly even notice the difference.

Later I kept repeating the revised line in my head: *like sneakers in a washer.* I tried to live with that line, but it didn't sound right. Maybe you aren't supposed to put sneakers in a dryer, but my mother always did. I still do it! What a racket they make—tumbling and slam-banging and ker-thumping away. Sneakers in a washing machine wouldn't make a noisy commotion. In fact, a washing machine would *silence* a pair of sneakers. That was exactly the wrong image. I had to do something about this.

Nervously I dialed my editor's number.

"I've been thinking—I really don't want to change that line," I said, and proceeded to explain why. There was a long pause on the other end.

"Hmmm," she finally said. "You know, in my apartment building there are warnings on the dryers in enormous red letters: DRYERS GET EXTREMELY HOT. DO NOT PUT ANY RUBBER MATERIAL IN DRYERS. So, maybe I overreacted. All right. Let's leave the line as is."

Revision depends on being able to reread what you have written. What works? What needs work? Where did I wander off the topic? Where do I need some examples or evidence to back up an argument?

"When I write something that interests me I go back," the poet William Stafford said. "When I write something that doesn't interest me, I go on."

I agree. I don't revise everything I write, and I think it's a mistake to insist that students revise. The decision about whether or not to revise is one of the choices every writer must make. If the student isn't invested in the piece, I think it's a mistake to force him to revise it. Rather, let him go on and work on a new piece of writing.

Too many students conceive of revision as a way to fix a broken piece. In fact, it's just the opposite—it's a way to honor a strong piece that has real potential.

"When I was in school and a teacher told me to revise, I thought that meant my writing was a broken-down car that needed to go to the repair shop," says Naomi Shihab Nye. "I felt insulted. I didn't realize the teacher was saying, 'Make it shine. It's worth it.' Now I see *revision* as a beautiful word of hope. It's a new vision of something. It means you don't have to be perfect the first time. What a relief!' "

In this chapter I'm focusing on revision in writing, but it applies to teaching, as well. When we work with students we, too, must be willing to reflect and reconsider. I am haunted by my writing conference with Rachita, the dead dog's footprints still visible in the sandbox. Sometimes when young writers say they don't want to revise, they are really saying that they don't know *how* to integrate the new image into the writing. Maybe I could have approached this conference in a different way:

"Wow, Rachita. That's the kind of image that poets work so hard to get. I've got a question for you: if you were going to add that image to your poem, would you want to put it in the beginning? The middle? The end? It's a powerful image, and I can show you how to include it."

In an article I wrote for *The New Advocate,* I compared the way my editors work with me to how teachers work with students. Of course, these relationships are not identical. As writing teachers we strive to "teach the writer, not the writing," as Lucy Calkins has said. Editors are not trying to teach me; their goal is to get the best possible finished product. Still, there are some intriguing parallels. In the *New Advocate* article I wondered: what conditions do my editors provide for me that allow me to successfully revise my work? How might writing teachers provide these conditions to our students? I came up with three crucial conditions:

1) **A skilled outside reader.**

Writing is very personal; I don't take suggestions from just anybody. My editors are skilled, literate readers with high standards. It's both a privilege and a challenge to write for them. Teachers, too, need to present ourselves as literate readers when we talk to students about their writing. They should see us as people who love language when it is used well.

Our students need to see us first as a *reader*—sharing our interest, delight, or occasional confusion—before we morph into our role as teacher. I would even go so far to say that in a conference we earn the right to teach by first dwelling *as a reader* in the student's writing.

2) **Someone who genuinely likes and respects my work.**

When my editors discuss my writing with me, they begin by giving specific examples of what works in the manuscript I'm working on. Like any kid, I lower my resistance/defensiveness when that happens. I'm most responsive to readers who are sympathetic to my vision, who try to stand in my shoes when they make a revision suggestion. Their general attitude is: "You're a wonderful writer, this is a great book, and I know with a little more work you can make it even better than it already is."

3) Give and take.

Editors typically wield greater power than an author, especially when the author is a novice. In "Won't You Come Home Bill Bailey?" my sense of relative powerless almost made me go along with a revision I didn't believe in. A classroom teacher operates from a position of power when he or she talks with students about their writing. It's important to defuse this power imbalance: through careful listening, humor, respect, and knowing when to back down (as I did with Rachita) when a writer strongly disagrees with a suggestion.

Young writers need us to respond to their work in the spirit of what they are trying to do. And they need teachers who respect their ownership of the writing. This phrase has fallen out of fashion in recent years, and maybe it has been used as too much of an absolute. But young writers still need what I need—a sense of being in control of their work, that it is theirs.

Bottom line: When a teacher suggests a revision, the student should have the final say over whether or not to make the change in their writing. We open the door, the student decides whether or not to step through. However, if a writing teacher can create an atmosphere that values risk-taking, students are more likely to experiment with revisions for their texts-in-progress.

Once, while having lunch with Donald Murray, I mentioned that I'd just received a very strange letter from a credit card company. They wanted to console me for the "loss" of my wife (who was, by the way, very much alive) and to remind me that I was responsible for her debt.

Don burst out laughing. "You've got to write about this!"

That idea hadn't crossed my mind. "You think I should?"

"Definitely!" he exclaimed.

So I went home and spent about ninety minutes writing a draft. At 2:30 I drove over to Don's house and dropped it in his mailbox. When I got home I called and invited him to make any suggestions as to how I might improve the manuscript. Here's the beginning of what I sent him.

DEATH AND REBIRTH IN THE CHANGE OF A NAME

In these modern times it's no big deal for people to alter essential elements of their identity: teeth, lip thickness, hair color.

Names, too. For women, changing a last name can be a way of defining identity, reclaiming ethnicity, or shedding an unwanted spouse. But it can also have unexpected consequences.

Before we were married my fiancée said she intended to keep her last name, Curtis, the family name of her ex-husband. This made sense to me. The woman I loved already had established a professional reputation in the field of education as "JoAnn Curtis." Then, too, there was the question of maternal loyalty; her two sons also bore that name.

Still, to me, JoAnn had never seemed wholly defined by an Anglo name like Curtis. Her pedigree runs three quarters Italian, one quarter Lebanese. She has deep brown eyes and an amazing shock of exuberant, sometimes unruly, dark hair. The joke between us is that each day she loses more hair to her hairbrush than I have left on my head.

A year ago, while working on a piece of autobiographical writing, JoAnn decided she wanted to take back her maiden name. I liked this move, much as I feared that yet another name on the mailbox might imperil the delivery of our mail. This new/old maiden name—Portalupi—seemed a much better fit. In Italian the exotic name means *carry the wolf*.

After my two stepsons gave cautious approval to her decision, JoAnn went to court, acquired the proper documents, and set out to alter the highway of documents that defines who we are: driver's license, credit cards, insurance beneficiaries. . . . Everything went swimmingly until last week when I received this startling letter from our credit card company:

"Dear Mr. Fletcher,

Thank you for contacting us concerning the above account. Please accept our sympathy in this time of loss. We know how difficult these times can be, therefore, we hope to make the processing of the account as easy as possible for you . . ."

The letter went on to ask for the exact date of death. I was asked to sign a statement whose wording was: "As a joint obligor, I understand I will be held responsible for the balance and a First Card representative will contact me regarding payment arrangements. Enclosed is a copy of the death certificate. Please accept this information within 30 days. Once again, please accept our sincere condolences."

The letter was signed by a woman named Janette Langer-strom from the "First Card Decedent Unit." There was also a phone number. My hands were shaking as I punched the digits.

"Yes?" a woman asked. "Account number, please?"

In a trembling voice I read the numbers.

"May I help you?"

"Yes, I just received a very peculiar letter," I said. . . .

(My piece continued for several more pages.)

Don read my draft immediately and telephoned me.

"It's pretty good, but it really starts on page two," he said. "The piece gets interesting when you receive the letter. I think that's your lead."

"Hm." I paused, trying to digest that. "What about the title?"

"Not great," he said, "but don't worry about that. That can be changed later."

I hung up the phone. After rereading my piece several times, I realized that Don was right. The first paragraphs of my piece would be boring to readers. So I spent another ninety minutes revising it and brought it back to Don.

At 5 P.M. (the same day Don and I had had lunch) the phone rang. It was Don, and he was calling with good news: he had faxed my piece to his editor at the *Boston Globe*. She liked the piece and wanted to buy it (for $800!) to use in the *Boston Globe Sunday Magazine*. I was thrilled. Here's how it appeared in print.

DEAD WRONG by Ralph Fletcher

When your credit-card company sends its condolences, you know you're in trouble

"Dear Mr. Fletcher," the letter from our credit-card company began, in-nocuously enough. "Thank you for contacting us concerning the above account. Please accept our sympathy in this time of loss. We know how difficult these times can be. Therefore, we hope to make the processing of the account as easy as possible for you . . ."

The letter went on to ask for my wife's exact date of death. I was also asked to sign a statement:

"As a joint obligor, I understand I will be held responsible for the [account] balance. . . . Enclosed is a copy of the death certificate . . ."

Story published by *The Boston Globe Magazine*, 1995.

The letter was signed by a woman named Janette Langerstrom from the "First Card Decedent Unit." There was also a phone number. With shaking hands, I punched in the digits.

"Account number, please?" a woman asked.

In a trembling voice, I read off the numbers.

"May I help you, Mr. Fletcher?"

"Yes. I just received this strange letter," I said. I went on to describe it. This was followed by a lengthy pause.

"How may I help you, Mr. Fletcher?" the woman asked politely.

"Well, in the first place, you can tell me why this letter got sent to me. This has nothing to do with me."

"Sir, are you married to JoAnn Curtis?" the woman asked. She had a tone of smug, practiced sympathy.

"Well, yes."

"Well, apparently your wife has died."

"Died?"

Another pause.

"You weren't aware of that?"

"No," I said.

"We have her death certificate here," the woman said. "When did you last see her?"

"About two hours ago."

"Oh." She sounded surprised and a bit disappointed.

"Let me get this straight," I said. "You've got a *death* certificate? For my wife?"

"Just a minute, sir," the woman said, less sure of herself now. "Can you hold a minute, please?"

I held, my head swirling with vertigo. My wife, dead? I thought of our four boys, who range in age from 13 to 2, who combine to polish off a loaf of bread and a gallon of milk daily. She'd better *not* be dead. What was this about? Why would someone pass out a fake death certificate for my wife? Of all the scams I had ever heard of, this was the sickest.

"Mr. Fletcher?" It was the woman's voice, softer, tinged with contrition. "I'm sorry. It seems there has been a mistake. Here's what happened. Has your wife recently changed her name?"

Story published by *The Boston Globe Magazine*, 1995.

"Yes."

"Well, the court document she sent in said at the top, 'Probate Court, State of New Hampshire.' I'm afraid someone here saw 'probate' and jumped to the conclusion that your wife had died."

"That's quite a leap."

"Yes. We're terribly sorry," she said. "Really. I hope this hasn't inconvenienced you."

I hung up the phone. What had died was no more, and no less, than my wife's identity as "JoAnn Curtis," the family name of her ex-husband. For five years she had kept it, having established a professional reputation in the field of education under that name. Then, too, sons also bore the name.

Still, to me, JoAnn had never seemed wholly embraced by an Anglo name like Curtis. Her pedigree runs three-quarters Italian, one-quarter Lebanese. She has deep brown eyes and an amazing shock of exuberant, sometimes unruly, dark hair. A joke between us is that each day she loses more hair to her hairbrush than I have left on my head.

A year ago, while working on a piece of autobiographical writing, JoAnn decided she wanted to take back her maiden name: Portalupi. I liked this move, much as I feared that yet another name on the mailbox might imperil the delivery of our mail. This new/old maiden name had an element of exotic mystery; in Italian the name means "carry the wolf."

After my two stepsons gave cautious approval, JoAnn went to court, acquired the proper documents, and set out to alter driver's license, credit cards, insurance beneficiaries, Social Security . . . Everything had gone without a glitch. Until now.

After a few deep breaths, I began to see this issue from the bank's point of view. It was clear that First Card had no particular interest in my emotional well-being. The company's condolences were only an excuse to get at its fundamental concern, which boiled down to: "Your wife is dead, but you are still responsible for her debt. Got that?"

I kept coming back to those six minutes and 35 seconds when I was on hold, suspended, my life stuck on PAUSE. The logical part of me, of course, knew that my wife was alive. Hadn't I kissed her goodbye just a couple of hours earlier? Hadn't she been wearing that flower-print

Story published by *The Boston Globe Magazine*, 1995.

dress she got at Stern's? But another part of me felt a tiny splinter of doubt. I knew credit-card companies had vast vaults of knowledge about us. Maybe the companies knew metaphysical things that I didn't. Maybe this was how these tragedies unfolded, the crazy phone call from out of the blue, the impossible news, the denial, that sickening sensation of free fall down an elevator shaft.

In the days that followed, this incident would metamorphose into a dicey story, a ripsnorting Ripley's believe-it-or-not. I wondered if in time this would become a piece of family lore—how Mom's rebirth as a Portalupi led to a mistaken case of her death. Maybe later we would be able to savor all the delicious ironies.

Whenever I have told people this story, they have laughed, sputtered, rolled their eyes. Oh, those jolly bank computers, what would they think of next? We would swap stories about the compounded absurdities of bureaucracy and technology. But what I could never fully communicate, even to my closest friends, was the quality of those eternal moments waiting on hold while a stranger sought to prove or disprove the existence of my wife.

Story published by *The Boston Globe Magazine*, 1995.

Un-Final Thoughts

Real writers serve their material. They allow it to
pass through them and have the opportunity to move
beyond the daily limitations of being inside themselves.
It's like being led by a whisper.

— JAYNE ANNE PHILLIPS

MY BROTHER JIM was a born naturalist. Once, when we were kids, he was exploring the woods with a bunch of fellow Boy Scouts. We spotted a small run-down shack that had caved in on one side. Jim got there first and clambered in. A moment later he emerged with a loud and exultant cry. What we saw made us gasp. He was holding two fistfuls of snakes! He had surprised them—garter snakes and grass snakes—sunning on an old piece of plywood. I will never forget the image of my brother, grinning like some modern Medusa, brandishing those snakes for everyone to see.

Isn't writing a little like that? The writer goes out into the world (or descends into the inner world) and returns with both fists clutching a mass of words, ideas, characters, places, stories, insights, arguments, possibly poisonous, hopefully not, and brandishes them, alive and squirming, before the startled reader.

Let me end this book with a few deep beliefs about writing that don't quite fit into the previous chapters.

Don't be afraid to live like a writer. Writers explore. There are two whole universes for you to explore—the one on the inside, and the physical one on the outside. Take your choice: inner or outer. Or best: both.

And I don't just mean exploring through words or books, though that's certainly important. I mean real exploration. "Don't let your books get in the way of your education," Mark Twain once said. In other words: live. Writers don't shy away from new experiences. If you have a chance to go somewhere new, go. Have an adventure. If you have a choice between watching a movie at home or helping out at a soup kitchen for homeless people, go to the soup kitchen, out of curiosity if nothing else.

Real exploration means that you'll probably get lost. That's all right. A famous naturalist once said that you cannot really know any wilderness until you have been truly and utterly lost in that wilderness. The same could be said for the wilderness of writing.

But don't fall into the trap of thinking you must live glamorously or dangerously in some exotic locale to be a writer, either. There are poems, plays, stories, articles, novels everywhere, right under your feet, just waiting to be written. Open your eyes and the rest of your senses. Look for them where you are right now. The German poet Rainer Maria Rilke put it this way:

> If your daily life seems poor, do not blame it; blame yourself, tell
> yourself that you are not poet enough to call forth its riches.

Think small. The best things to write about are often the tiniest things—your brother's junk drawer, something weird your dog once did, changing a dirty diaper, the moment you realized you were too old to take a bath with your brother. James Michener has written a marvelous essay about writing: "Go Waste, Young Man." Michener, who didn't start writing seriously until he was forty, found that the "in-between" jobs—washing dishes, working at an unemployment office—were the ones he drew upon most as a writer.

Listen to people. Listen to their stories, to how they tell those stories, where they put the emphasis. Not just young people but old people, too. Old people are walking history books. These men and women have incredible stories, and most will tell them if you will listen. Young people can tell us of life's plans and hopes, but old people can tell us what life can do to those hopes.

Have courage. Who among us was born with the genius of a Steve Jobs or the athletic gifts of a Michael Jordan? Nobody I know. But I do know people with real guts, who will stand up for what they believe in. Courage is a quality available to all of us. Speak up. Let the voice in your writing be heard.

Writing is powerful stuff. Ralph Nader's book *Unsafe At Any Speed* forced the auto industry to make drastic changes in car design. *Half The Sky: Turning Oppression Into Opportunity for Women Worldwide*, a book by Nicholas Kristof and Sheryl YuDunn, shined a powerful light on the sex slave industry and led to concrete reforms. The world has been altered forever by writers and the books they created. Don't be afraid to write about the wrongs and injustices of the world as you see them.

On the other hand, sometimes a writer must keep silent. James Joyce identified "silence, exile, cunning" as essential tools of a writer. There is a part of the writer's consciousness that stands apart, observing, reflecting. Some writing never gets shared. Certain ideas must grow very slowly inside you— you've got to give them time and room to grow. For the past twenty years I have had this idea for a book. I won't talk about it here—I am not ready to share it. And I can't write it. Not yet. I'm trying to grow into it. Someday I hope to write that book.

> There's no shortcut. Writing is hard.
> Live in the concrete world. Wiretap your inner voice.

THE RISE OF DIGITAL WRITING

The writing world has certainly changed a great deal since this book was first published twenty years ago. It was a pre-email, pre-Facebook, pre-Twitter era, long before people sat in meetings listening to one person while madly texting someone else. Back then if you had told me that people would one day store their writing in the cloud, well, I would have burst out laughing. Today we inhabit a new world of electronic or "digital" writing. This is a rich subject, well worth a book in itself (*The Digital Writing Workshop* by Troy Hicks is a good place to start), but I would like to highlight a few ways the digital world has impacted writing, both in and out of school.

- **Ease.** Don't happen to have your special pen or nifty little notebook with you when it's time to write? No problem. You can easily write on your smartphone, iPad, laptop, Kindle, or work computer. Most of today's new techno-gizmos come with a keyboard. Writing tools are becoming more and more ubiquitous. This is bad news for procrastinators—there are fewer and fewer excuses for not writing!

  Once upon a time a poet needed to have a quill pen, ink, parchment paper, and a crackling fire (plus a tamed raven) in order to write a poem. How far we have come from that world! Last night, while flying home, I flipped open my MacBook Pro and tried several drafts of a poem. First I tried writing it with four three-line stanzas, then with three four-line stanzas, and finally with six two-line stanzas. The computer allowed me to quickly manipulate text, stanzas, and line breaks.

- **Audience/publishing.** The Internet has created a more democratic world for writing and has made it much easier for writers to find an audience. Today, with very little difficulty, you can self-publish your own novel either as a paper product or an e-book. The digital world has made writers, editors, and agents more accessible. We also see these changes in writing classrooms. A class of sixth graders can create an online literary magazine and send out the link so readers around the world can read their poems. I get emails from kids around the world, many of whom include one of their poems or stories for me to read. The prospect of having real readers can motivate kids to revise and edit their work.

- **More flexible formats.** People today "write" in many new modes, with more springing up all the time. Kids create electronic portfolios. They send words accompanied by photographs, video, music, or podcasts. Ryan, an eighth grade boy from Machaisport, Maine, sent me a powerful YouTube video titled "The Abandonment of Maine." I would argue that words still make up the core of writing; nevertheless the writing world has undeniably become much more visual and much less word-centric.

- **Social.** Most novelists and poets still work alone, as they always have. But in many arenas, writing has become less solitary and more collaborative. In the good old days, I'd mail a manuscript off to my agent and wait at least a week for a response. Now I email it to her in the morning and often get her feedback by the afternoon. Writers expect and receive instant responses to their text messages. Writers who live thousands of miles apart can use a program like Google Docs to co-construct the same document in real time.

In many cases, students may be using forms of digital writing before we are even aware of them. Thus it's becoming more and more important for teachers (many of whom are "digital immigrants," as I am) to become aware of what kind of digital literacy kids are using outside the classroom.

This new digital world can seem overwhelming, but it's important to remember that strong writing is still strong writing. *Writing is no more, and no less, than putting particular words in a particular order to create the effect you want to create.* The coolest graphics or wildest flash video cannot rescue drab, lifeless writing. A columnist who works for ESPN or the Huffington Post still must write lively, anecdotal, engaging prose if she wants readers to continue reading what she has to say. Whether I use parchment paper or a computer, I still must select the right words and craft them in such a way to make the poem work.

Returning to this book has brought unexpected pleasure, like reconnecting with a dear friend who has been out of your life too long. I've enjoyed holding these sentences in my hand, letting the spirit and the language run through my fingers again. In the first edition of this book I named this last chapter "Final Thoughts," a title that now strikes me as somewhat presumptuous, and so I decided to un-final it. Learning to write is an ongoing journey with no clear-cut destination—there's no "there" there. I will never stop learning how to become a better writer.

MY LATEST THOUGHTS ABOUT WRITING

1) "Write about what makes you different." (Sandra Cisneros)
2) Set your own standard and hold yourself accountable to it. When I have a strong line or two, I set that as the standard and try to make the rest of the manuscript worthy of it.
3) Write small. The devil is in the details.
4) Don't "overmix the batter." Revision is a crucial part of the process, but beware of revising the life out of a piece.
5) Develop an internal sense for what makes good writing. Don't let others be the final arbiters of what you write.
6) "Feed the dragon," Don Murray advised. "Do the writing only you really want to do."
7) Beware the electric fence. It zaps you once and causes you to pull back forever, never to test it again. Be brave. Write the unspeakable.
8) Use a writer's notebook to collect lots of random stuff. You never know what might come in handy.
9) Violate the expected. Strong writing contains surprise: a fresh phrase, strange idea, or unexpected plot development.
10) Keep reading. Kafka describes a book as the "axe for the frozen sea within us." Not all readers are writers, but all writers are readers.
11) Forgive yourself for not being able to write like Milan Kundera or Sandra Cisneros, but. . . .
12) Don't be afraid to set high goals for yourself.

Growing up, my favorite short story was titled "The Five-Dollar Job," about a boy who gets a job cutting a woman's lawn. The woman explains that she will pay him according to the quality of his work. An average job will earn you two dollars and fifty cents, she tells him. A good job is around three dollars, three-fifty for a very good job, a four-dollar job is just about perfect and, as for the five-dollar job, well, that's just about impossible: It's never been done so it's not worth talking about.

The boy takes the job. Week after week, he cuts her lawn. After he finishes, he surveys the yard and gives the woman an honest appraisal.

"Three dollars," he says the first week.

"Three-fifty," he says the next, and so on. The woman never quarrels with his price.

As the summer wears on he settles into the three dollar to three-fifty range with one or two lapses to two-fifty. But at night he dreams of the five-dollar job. It haunts him. He can't get it out of his mind. He tries picturing it, imagining the work necessary to complete such a feat. Every Saturday he begins with high hopes, but every time his will weakens and he falls short.

One Saturday he arrives at her house early and determined. He uses a rolling pin to smooth down all the wormholes. This task nearly knocks out his energy but on that day he discovers a secret: the catnap. He lies down and naps beneath one of her trees. When he wakes up ten minutes later he feels totally refreshed. Back to work. He cuts the lawn twice, first one way, then another, the way they do it at major league baseball stadiums. He adds a dozen other extra touches (interspersed with another catnap) until that lawn fairly sparkles. Twilight has begun to fall when he knocks on the woman's door.

"How much this week?" she asks him.

"Five dollars, ma'am," he replies without hesitation.

"I thought I said the five-dollar job was impossible."

"I know you did," he answers her. "But I just did it."

She pauses and looks at him closely.

"Well, if this is the first five-dollar job in history," she finally says, "I guess it's worth taking a look at."

They walked the lawn together. Even he is amazed at how stunningly beautiful it looks. The woman turns to look at him.

"Young man, you did something great today."

Writing about writing always leaves me with an intense thirst to write about something else. As I reach the end of this book, I can feel all sorts of poems, stories, and novels tugging at my mind's sleeve. If this book inspires anyone else to write, well then, I'll consider it a job well done.

APPENDIX

WORD PLAY

Pyrotechnics on the Page: Playful Craft That Sparks Writing, by Ralph Fletcher (Stenhouse)

Puns and Games: Jokes, Riddles, Daffynitions, Tairy Fales, Rhymes, and More Word Play for Kids, by Richard Lederer (Chicago Review Press)

Eats, Shoots and Leaves: The Zero Tolerance Approach to Punctuation, by Lynn Truss (Gotham)

For Young Readers and Writers

Mr. Putney's Quacking Dog, Jon Agee (Michael di Capua Books). Also *Palindromania!* (Farrar, Straus and Giroux)

Things that Are Most in the World, by Judi Barrett (Atheneum Books for Young Readers)

Chicken Cheeks, by Michael Black (Simon & Schuster)

Grammar: The Bill of Writes, by Mary Budzik (Kingfisher, Basher Basics Series)

You Are What You Eat and Other Mealtime Hazards, by Serge Bloch (Sterling)

"Slowly, Slowly, Slowly," said the Sloth, by Eric Carle (Puffin)

Once Upon a Twice, by Denise Doyen (Random House)

The Word Snoop: A Wild and Witty Tour of the English Language! by Ursula Dubosarsky (Dial Books)

Miss Alaineus: A Vocabulary Disaster, by Debra Frasier (Sandpiper)

The King Who Reigned, by Fred Gwynne (Aladdin)

Merry-Go-Round: A Book About Nouns and *Kites Sail High: A Book About Verbs,* by Ruth Heller (Puffin). Also *Many Luscious Lollipops: A Book About Adjectives* and *A Cache of Jewels: And Other Collective Nouns*

The Weighty Word Book, by Paul M. Levitt, Douglas A. Burger, and Elissa S. Guralnick (Roberts Rinehart)

Monkey Business, by Wallace Edwards (Kids Can Press, Ltd.)

Eat Your Words: A Fascinating Look at the Language of Food, by Charlotte Foltz Jones (Delacorte Books for Young Readers)

Punished, by David Lubar (Darby Creek)

Gimme Cracked Corn and I Will Share, by Kevin O'Malley (Walker)

Chicken Butt and *Chicken Butt's Back!* by Erica S. Perl (Abrams Books for Young Readers)

Punctuation Takes a Vacation, by Robin Pulver (Holiday House)

Al Pha's Bet, by Amy Krouse Rosenthal (Putnam Juvenile). Also *Spoon* (Hyperion)

Runny Babbit: A Billy Sook, by Shel Silverstein (HarperCollins)

The Great Fuzz Frenzy, by Janet Stevens (Harcourt)

Once There Was a Bull . . . (frog), by Rick Walton, also *Bullfrog Pops!* (Gibbs Smith)

The Pig in the Spigot, by Richard Wilbur (Sandpiper)

Tough Cookie, by David Wisniewski (HarperCollins)

A First Thesaurus, by Harriet Wittels and Joan Greisman (Golden Books)

Poetry

Dinothesaurus: Prehistoric Poems and Paintings, by Douglas Florian, also *Poetrees, UnBEElievables: Honeybee Poems and Paintings* (and many others) (Beach Lane Books)

Countdown to Summer: A Poem for Every Day of the School Year, by J. Patrick Lewis (Little, Brown Books for Young Readers)

Lemonade: and Other Poems Squeezed from a Single Word, by Bob Raczka (Roaring Brook Press)

MEMOIRS

My Father's Summers: A Daughter's Memoir, by Kathi Appelt (Holt)

A Grain of Wheat: A Writer Begins, by Clyde Robert Bulla (Boyds Mill Press)

A Girl From Yamhill, by Beverly Cleary (HarperCollins)

My Reading Life, by Pat Conroy (Nan A. Talese)

King of the Mild Frontier: An Ill-Advised Autobiography, by Chris Crutcher (Greenwillow)

Boy: Tales of Childhood, by Roald Dahl (Puffin)

Marshfield Dreams: When I Was a Kid, by Ralph Fletcher (Henry Holt)

Homesick: My Own Story, by Jean Fritz (Puffin Modern Classics)

On Writing: A Memoir of the Craft, by Stephen King (Scribner)

Bird by Bird: Some Instructions on Writing and Life and *Travelling Mercies: Some Thoughts on Faith* (Anchor), *Operating Instructions* (Ballantine Books), and *Some Assembly Required* (Riverhead) by Anne Lamott

Starting from Home: A Writer's Beginnings, by Milton Meltzer (iUniverse)

How I Came to Be a Writer, by Phyllis R. Naylor (Atheneum Books for Young Readers)

Bill Peet: An Autobiography, by Bill Peet (Houghton Mifflin)

Knucklehead, by Jon Scieszka (Viking)

For Older Readers

I Know Why the Caged Bird Sings, by Maya Angelou (Random House)

A Place to Stand, by Jimmy Santiago Baca (Grove Press)

Growing Up, by Russell Baker (Penguin Group USA)

No Name in the Street, by James Baldwin (Vintage) and *Go Tell It on the Mountain,* by James Baldwin (Random House)

Dancing With Max: A Mother and Son Who Broke Free, by Emily Colson (Zondervan)

Lift and *The Middle Place,* by Kelly Corrigan (Voice)

Stop-Time: A Memoir, by Frank Conroy (Penguin USA)

An American Childhood, by Annie Dillard (HarperCollins)

Following Ezra: What One Father Learned About Gumby, Otters, Autism, and Love from His Extraordinary Son, by Tom Fields-Meyer (NAL Trade)

How to Write Your Life Story, by Ralph Fletcher (HarperCollins)

The Open Door: When Writers First Learned to Read, by Steven Gilbar (David R. Godine)

Hole in My Life, by Jack Gantos (Farrar, Straus and Giroux)

Strive Toward Freedom: The Montgomery Story, by Martin Luther King, Jr. (HarperCollins)

Kaffir Boy: An Autobiography, by Mark Mathabane (Free Press)

Until Tuesday, by Luis Carlos Montalvan (Hyperion)

The Last Lecture, by Randy Pausch and Jeffrey Zaslow (Hyperion)

One Writer's Beginnings, by Eudora Welty (Harvard University Press)

Black Boy, by Richard Wright (HarperCollins)

Inventing the Truth: The Art and Craft of Memoir, by William Zinsser (Houghton Mifflin Harcourt)

This Boy's Life: A Memoir, by Tobias Wolff (Grove Press)

SOME NOTABLE BEGINNINGS

1. One day last spring, Louis, a butcher, turned into a fish. Silvery scales. Big lips. A tail. A salmon.
   Louis the Fish, by Arthur Yorinks (Square Fish)

2. Leonardo was a terrible monster . . .
   He couldn't scare anyone.
   Leonardo, the Terrible Monster, by Mo Willems (Hyperion)

3. And how's my little girl?
   Granpa, by John Burningham (Red Fox)

4. It was in the summer of the year when the relatives came. They came up from Virginia. They left when their grapes were nearly purple enough to pick, but not quite.

The Relatives Came, by Cynthia Rylant (Atheneum Books for
Young Readers)

5. Guts! Brains! Eyeballs!
"Take that. You're dead," said Fred Zombie.
"I'm not dead. I'm *un*-dead," said Voodoo Zombie.
Stink and Webster were playing Attack of the Knitting Needle Zombies
when Fred Zombie's eye fell off and rolled across the floor.
Stink and the Midnight Zombie Walk, by Megan McDonald
(Candlewick Press)

6. Here is James Henry Trotter when he was about four years old.
Up until this time, he had had a happy life, living peacefully with his mother
and father in a beautiful house beside the sea. There were always plenty of
other children for him to play with, and there was the sandy beach for him
to run about on, and the ocean to paddle in. It was the perfect life for a
small boy.
  Then, one day, James' mother and father went to London to do some
shopping, and there a terrible thing happened. Both of them suddenly got
eaten up (in full daylight, mind you, and on a crowded street) by an enormous angry rhinoceros which had escaped from the London Zoo
James and the Giant Peach, by Roald Dahl (Puffin)

7. Once upon a time there was a bat—a little light brown bat, the color of
coffee with cream in it. He looked like a furry mouse with wings.
The Bat-Poet, by Randall Jarrell (HarperCollins)

8. His mother was ugly and his father was ugly, but Shrek was uglier than the
two of them put together.
Shrek! by William Steig (Farrar, Straus and Giroux)

9. I will always remember when the stars fell down around me and lifted me
up above the George Washington Bridge.
Tar Beach, by Faith Ringgold (Random House Children's Books)

10. The day I decided to steal a dog was the same day my best friend,
Luanne Godfrey, found out I lived in a car.
How to Steal a Dog, by Barbara O'Connor (Square Fish)

11. I know I'm not an ordinary ten-year-old kid. I mean, sure, I do ordinary
things. I eat ice cream. I ride my bike. I play ball. I have an Xbox. Stuff like
that makes me ordinary. I guess. And I feel ordinary. Inside. But I know ordinary kids don't make other ordinary kids run away screaming in playgrounds.

I know ordinary kids don't get stared at wherever they go.
Wonder, by R. J. Palacio (Alfred A. Knopf)

12. Owen Jester tiptoed across the gleaming linoleum floor and slipped the frog into the soup.

   It swam gracefully under the potatoes, pushing its froggy legs through the pale yellow broth. It circled the carrots and bumped into the celery and finally settled beside a parsnip, its bulging eyes staring up at Owen.
The Fantastic Secret of Owen Jester, by Barbara O'Connor (Farrar, Straus and Giroux)

13. Mickey Cray had been out of work ever since a dead iguana fell from a palm tree and hit him on the head.
Chomp, by Carl Hiassen (Knopf Books for Young Readers)

14. The best time to talk to ghosts is just before the sun comes up. That's when they can hear us true, Momma said. That's when ghosts can answer us.
Chains, by Laurie Halse Anderson (Atheneum Books for Young Readers)

15. Late in the winter of my seventeenth year, my mother decided I was depressed, presumably because I rarely left the house, spent quite a lot of time in bed, read the same book over and over, ate infrequently, and devoted quite a bit of my abundant free time to thinking about death.
The Fault in Our Stars, by John Green (Dutton)

16. It was Big Poops who first suggested the idea.
Also Known As Rowan Pohi, by Ralph Fletcher (Clarion)

ENDINGS

Surprise Endings in Picture Books

Charlie Anderson, by Barbara Abercrombie (Margaret K. McElderry Books)

Just Like Daddy, by Frank Asch (for young children) (Aladdin)

Extra Yarn, by Mac Barnett (Balzer + Bray)

The Wednesday Surprise, by Eve Bunting (Houghton Mifflin Harcourt)

I Want My Hat Back, by Jon Klassen (Candlewick Press)

Snow Day! by Lester Laminack (Peachtree)

My Bear Grizz, by Suzanne McGinness (Francis Lincoln Children's Books)

Flossie and the Fox, by Patricia C. McKissack (Penguin Group USA)

Stephanie's Ponytail, by Robert Munsch (Annick Press). Also *Thomas' Snowsuit* (Annikins)

In the Attic, by Hiawyn Oram (Andersen Press, Limited)

Huff & Puff: Can You Blow Down the Houses of the Three Little Pigs?, by Claudia Rueda (Abrams Appleseed)

Me Want Pet, by Tammi Sauer (Simon & Schuster)

The Frog Prince, by Jon Scieszka (Penguin Group USA)

The Sweetest Fig, by Chris Van Allsburg (Houghton Mifflin)

I Love My New Toy, by Mo Willems (Walker Books). Also *Should I Share My Ice Cream?*

Bear Wants More, by Karma Wilson (Margaret K. McElderry Books)

Surprise Endings Novels and Short Stories

No Talking, by Andrew Clements (Simon & Schuster)

The Gift of the Magi, by O. Henry (Candlewick)

Circular Endings in Picture Books

Very Last First Time, by Jan Andrews (Groundwood Books)

No Jumping on the Bed, by Tedd Arnold (Dial Books for Young Readers). Also *No More Water in the Tub!* (Puffin)

Grandfather Twilight, by Barbara Berger (Penguin Group USA)

If You Give a Mouse a Cookie series, by Laura Joffe Numeroff (HarperCollins)

The Relatives Came, by Cynthia Rylant (Atheneum Books for Young Readers)

Two Bad Ants, by Chris Van Allsburg (Houghton Mifflin)

Louis the Fish, by Arthur Yorinks (Square Fish)

Circular Endings in Novels

Pictures of Hollis Woods, by Patricia Reilly Giff (Wendy Lamb Books)

Flowers for Algernon, by Daniel Keyes (Houghton Mifflin Harcourt)

A Wrinkle in Time, by Madeleine L'Engle (Square Fish)

The Hobbit: or There and Back Again, by J. R. R. Tolkien (Houghton Mifflin Harcourt)

Poignant Endings in Picture Books

The Two of Them, by Aliki (HarperCollins)

Bink and Gollie, by Kate DiCamillo, Alison McGhee (Candlewick Press)

Wilfred Gordon McDonald Partridge, by Mem Fox (Kane/Miller)

Little White Rabbit, by Kevin Henkes (Greenwillow Press). Also *Wemberly Worried* and *Penny and Her Song*

The Year of the Perfect Christmas Tree, by Gloria Houston (Penguin Group USA)

Crow Call, by Lois Lowry (Scholastic Press)

The Keeping Quilt, by Patricia Polacco (Aladdin). Also *Thank You, Mr. Falker*

A Sick Day for Amos McGee, by Philip C. Stead (Roaring Book Press)

Faithful Elephants, by Yukio Tsuchiya (Houghton Mifflin Harcourt)

A Father Like That, by Charlotte Zolotow (HarperCollins). Also *William's Doll* (Perfection Learning)

Poignant Endings in Novels, Short Stories, and Memoirs

On My Honor, by M. D. Bauer (Random House Children's Books)

Sadako and the Thousand Paper Cranes, by Eleanor Coerr (Penguin Group USA)

Eight Plus One, by Robert Cormier (Random House Books for Children)

The Mighty Miss Malone, by Christopher Paul Curtis (Wendy Lamb Books)

The Miraculous Journey of Edward Tulane, by Kate DiCamillo (Candlewick)

Marshfield Dreams: When I Was a Kid, by Ralph Fletcher (Holt)

Throwing Shadows, short stories by E. L. Konigsburg (Aladdin)

Wonder, by R. J. Palacio (Knopf Books for Young Readers)

Bridge to Terabithia, by Katherine Paterson (HarperCollins)

A Dog's Way Home, by Bobbie Pyron (HarperCollins)

"Slower Than the Rest," short story in *Every Living Thing,* by Cynthia Rylant (Atheneum)

Ambiguous Endings

Where the Forest Meets the Sea, by Jeannie Baker (HarperCollins)

Granpa, by John Burningham (Square Fish)

I Want My Hat Back, by Jon Klassen (Candlewick Press)

BOOKS WITH STRONG CHARACTERS

Picture Books

The Two of Them, by Aliki (HarperCollins)

The Song and Dance Man, by Karen Ackerman (Random House Children's Books)

Granpa, by John Burningham (Red Fox)

Mollie's Pilgrim, by Barbara Cohen (HarperCollins)

Miss Rumphius, by Barbara Cooney (Penguin Group USA)

Bink and Gollie, by Kate DiCamillo and Alison McGhee (Candlewick Press)

Bella and Bean, by Rebecca Kai Dotlich (Atheneum Books for Young Readers)

Lilly's Purple Plastic Purse, by Kevin Henkes (HarperCollins). Also *Lilly's Big Day; Chester's Way; Chrysanthemum;* and *Sheila Rae, the Brave*

Tales of a Gambling Grandma, by Dayal Kaur Khalsa (Tundra Books)

Tacky the Penguin series, by Helen Lester (Houghton Mifflin Harcourt)

Through Grandpa's Eyes, by Patricia MacLachlan (HarperCollins)

Fancy Nancy series, by Jane O'Connor (HarperCollins)

The Recess Queen, by Alexis O'Neill (Scholastic)

Many books by William Steig, including *Amos and Boris* (Square Fish)

Elephant and Piggie series, by Mo Willems (Walker Books)

Crow Boy, by Taro Yashima (Penguin Group USA)

Books by Arthur Yorinks, including *Hey, Al* and *Louis the Fish*

I Know a Lady, by Charlotte Zolotow (HarperCollins). Also *William's Doll*

Novels with Strong Characters

Go Ask Alice, anonymous (Simon Pulse)

Tuck Everlasting, by Natalie Babbitt (Square Fish)

The Stories Julian Tells and *More Stories Julian Tells,* by Ann Cameron (Random House Children's Books)

Frindle, by Andrew Clements (Atheneum)

Hunger Games, by Suzanne Collins (Scholastic). Also *Catching Fire* and *Mockingjay*

"The Mustache" in *Eight Plus One,* by Robert Cormier (Random House Books for Children)

Elijah of Buxton, by Christopher Paul Curtis (Scholastic Press)

Charlie and the Chocolate Factory and *Matilda,* by Roald Dahl (Penguin Group USA)

Because of Winn Dixie, by Kate DiCamillo (Candlewick)

Flying Solo, by Ralph Fletcher (Sandpiper). Also *Spiderboy* and *Fig Pudding.*

Joey Pigza Swallowed the Key, by Jack Gantos (Farrar, Straus and Giroux)

The Fault in Our Stars, by John Green (Dutton Juvenile)

The Outsiders, by S. E. Hinton (Penguin Group USA)

Bunnicula: A Rabbit-Tale of Mystery, by Deborah and James Howe (Atheneum Books for Young Readers)

Books by Jack London, especially *White Fan* and *The Call of the Wild*

Hey World, Here I Am! by Jean Little (HarperCollins)

Autumn Street, by Lois Lowry (Random House Books for Children)

Gooney Bird Greene series, by Lois Lowry (Yearling and Houghton Mifflin)

Stink series, by Megan McDonald (Candlewick Press)

The Brilliant Fall of Gianna Z., by Kate Messner (Bloomsbury Publishing USA). Also *Sugar and Ice* and *The Marty McGuire* series

Anything by Katherine Paterson, especially *The Great Gilly Hopkins* and *Bridge to Terabithia*

Clementine series, by Sara Pennypacker (Scholastic)

The Lightning Thief, by Rick Riordan (Hyperion)

The Mostly True Adventures of Homer P. Figg, by Rodman Philbrick (Scholastic). Also *Freak The Mighty* (Scholastic)

Wednesday Wars and *OK for Now,* by Gary D. Schmidt (Houghton Mifflin Harcourt)

Maniac Magee and *Stargirl,* by Jerry Spinelli (Knopf)

Hound Dog True, by Linda Urban (Houghton Mifflin Harcourt)

Novels with Strong Characters for Older Readers

Cold Sassy Tree, by Olive Ann Burns (Dial)

Mrs. Bridge and *Mr. Bridge,* by Evan S. Connell (North Point Press)

Yellow Raft in Blue Water, by Michael Dorris (Warner)

The Sportswriter, by Richard Ford (Vintage)

The Kite Runner, by Khaled Hosseni (Riverhead)

The World According to Garp, by John Irving (Modern Library)

One Flew Over the Cuckoo's Nest, by Ken Kesey. Also *Sometimes a Great Notion* (Penguin Classics)

Interpreter of Maladies, by Jhumpa Lahiri (Mariner Books)

Love in the Time of Cholera, by Gabriel García Márquez (Vintage)

The Member of the Wedding, by Carson McCullers (Mariner Books)

Brightness Falls, by Jay McInerney (Vintage)

The Post-Birthday World, by Lionel Shriver (Harper Perennial)

Angle of Repose, by Wallace Stegner (Penguin)

VOICE

Picture Books

The Pain and the Great One, by Judy Blume (Random House Children's Books)

Bink and Gollie, by Kate DiCamillo and Alison McGhee (Candlewick Press)

On the Day You Were Born, by Debra Frasier (Houghton Mifflin Harcourt)

Tight Times, by Barbara Shook Hazen (Penguin Group USA)

Books by Bill Martin Jr. and John Archambault, especially *White Dynamite and Curly Kidd* (Henry Holt) and *Knots on a Counting Rope* (Square Fish)

The Keeping Quilt, by Patricia Polacco (Aladdin). Also *My Rotten Redheaded Older Brother* and *Pink and Say*

I Must Have Bobo! by Eileen Rosenthal (Atheneum)

Books by Cynthia Rylant, especially *The Relatives Came* (Atheneum Books for Young Readers) and *When I Was Young in the Mountains* (Penguin Group USA)

The True Story of the Three Little Pigs, by Jon Scieszka (Penguin Group USA)

Gila Monsters Meet You at the Airport, by Marjorie Sharmat (Aladdin)

It's a Book, by Lane Smith (Roaring Brook Press), also *John, Paul, George & Ben* (Hyperion)

Interrupting Chicken, by David Ezra Stein (Candlewick)

No, David! by David Shannon (Blue Sky Press)

Stevie, by Jon Steptoe (HarperCollins)

Dear Mrs. LaRue: Letters from Obedience School, by Mark Teague and *Detective LaRue: Letters from the Investigation* (Scholastic Press), also *Letters from the Campaign Trail: LaRue for Mayor* (Blue Sky Press)

Elephants Cannot Dance! by Mo Willems (Hyperion)

Short Stories and Novels

Black Elk Speaks: Being the Life Story of a Holy Man of the Oglala Sioux, by Nicholas Black Elk and John G. Neihardt (University of Nebraska Press)

The Absolutely True Diary of a Part-time Indian, by Sherman Alexie (Hachette)

How Lamar's Bad Prank Won a Bubba-Sized Trophy, by Crystal Allen (Balzer + Bray)

The Buddy Files series, by Dori Hillestad Butler (Albert Whitman and Company)

Because of Mr. Terupt, by Rob Buyea (Yearling)

The Education of Little Tree, by Forrest Carter (University of New Mexico Press)

Anything by Roald Dahl, for example *Boy* (Penguin)

The Trouble with Chickens, by Doreen Cronin (Balzer + Bray). Also *The Legend of Diamond Lil*

Out of My Mind, by Sharon Draper (Atheneum)

Love Medicine, by Louise Erdrich (HarperCollins)

Mockingbird, by Kathryn Erskine (Puffin)

Fig Pudding, by Ralph Fletcher (Dell) and *Also Known as Rowan Pohi* (Clarion Books) and *The One O'Clock Chop* (Henry Holt)

All I Really Need to Know I Learned in Kindergarten, pages 13–16, by Robert Fulghum (Random House Publishing Group)

Stupid Fast, by Geoff Herbach (Sourcebooks Fire)

The Defense of Thaddeus A. Ledbetter, by John Gosselink (Amulet Books)

That Was Then, This Is Now, by S. E. Hinton (Penguin Group USA)

Flowers for Algernon, by Daniel Keyes (Houghton Mifflin Harcourt)

Autumn Street, by Lois Lowry (Random House Children's Books)

So Much to Tell You, by John Marsden (Random House Publishing Group)

Greetings from Nowhere, by Barbara O'Connor (Farrar, Straus and Giroux)

Wonder, by R. J. Palacios (Knopf Books for Young Readers)

The Mostly True Adventures of Homer P. Figg, by Rodman Philbrick (Scholastic)

Becoming Naomi Leon, by Pam Munoz Ryan (Scholastic)

The Catcher in the Rye, by J. D. Salinger (Little Brown and Company)

A Taste of Blackberries, by Doris B. Smith (HarperCollins)

Moon Over Manifest, by Clare Vanderpool (Yearling)

Night, by Elie Wiesel (Farrar, Straus and Giroux)

Stanford Wong Flunks Big Time, by Lisa Yee (Scholastic), also *Millicent Min: Girl Genius* and *So Totally Emily Ebers*

Nonfiction Picture Books

A Medieval Feast, by Aliki (HarperCollins)

Where the Forest Meets the Sea, by Jeannie Baker (HarperCollins)

Mammoths and Mastodons: Titans of the Ice Age, by Cheryl Bardoe (Abrams)

The Periodic Table: Elements with Style! by Simon Basher (Kingfisher, Basher Basics Series)

Books by Byrd Baylor, including *The Way to Start the Day* (Aladdin Books)

A River Ran Wild and *The Great Kapok Tree,* by Lynne Cherry (Houghton Mifflin Harcourt)

The Magic School Bus series, by Joanna Cole (Scholastic)

Mermaid Queen: The Spectacular True Story of Annette Kellerman, Who Swam Her Way To Fame, Fortune & Swimsuit History! by Shana Corey, also *Here Come the Girl Scouts.* And *You Forgot Your Skirt, Amelia Bloomer* (Scholastic Press)

Nubs: The True Story of a Mutt, a Marine, and a Miracle, by Brian Dennis, Mary Nethery, and Kirby Larson (Little Brown)

The Popcorn Book and *The Cloud Book,* by Tomie dePaola (Holiday House)

Time Train, by Paul Fleischman (HarperCollins)

Moonshot: The Flight of Apollo 11, by Brian Floca (Atheneum/Richard Jackson Books)

Box Turtle at Long Pond, by William T. George (HarperCollins)

Ox-Cart Man, by Donald Hall (Penguin Group USA)

Owen and Mzee: The True Story of a Remarkable Friendship, by Craig Hatkoff, Peter Greste, and Paula Kahumbu (Scholastic)

Can We Save the Tiger? by Martin Jenkins (Candlewick)

Down, Down, Down: A Journey to the Bottom of the Ocean, by Steve Jenkins (Houghton Mifflin). Also: *Bones* and *Actual Size*

Seeds of Change: Wangari's Gift to the World, by Jen Cullerton Johnson (Lee and Low)

The Extraordinary Mark Twain (According to Susy), by Barbara Kerley (Scholastic)

A Prairie Boy's Winter, by William Kurelek (Houghton Mifflin Harcourt)

The Philharmonic Gets Dressed, by Karla Kuskin (HarperCollins)

The Shocking Truth About Energy, by Loreen Leedy (Holiday House)

The Year of Goodbyes: A True Story of Friendship, Family and Farewells, by Debbie Levy (Hyperion Books)

Heart and Soul: The Story of America and African Americans, by Kadir Nelson (Balzer + Bray). Also *We Are the Ship: The Story of the Negro Baseball Leagues* (Hyperion)

Ain't Nothing But a Man: My Quest to Find the Real John Henry, by Scott Reynolds Nelson (National Geographic Children's Books)

Dinosaur Mountain: Digging Into the Jurassic Age, by Deborah Kogan Ray (Farrar, Straus and Giroux)

Books by David M. Schwartz, including *How Much Is a Million?* (HarperCollins). Also *G Is for Googol* and *Q Is for Quark* (Dragonfly Books)

Hot Diggity Dog: The History of the Hot Dog, by Adrienne Sylver (Dutton Juvenile)

Henry Aaron's Dreams, by Matt Tavares (Candlewick)

Nettie's Trip South, by Ann Turner (Aladdin)

Moses: When Harriet Tubman Led Her People to Freedom, by Carole Boston Weatherford (Hyperion)

Nonfiction Picture Books for Younger Readers

A Snake Is Totally Tail, by Judi Barrett (Aladdin Books)

Caroline Arnold's Animals series, including *A Killer Whale's World, A Polar Bear's World, A Wombat's World* (Picture Window Books)

Books by Eric Carle, including *The Very Hungry Caterpillar* and *The Very Busy Spider* (Penguin)

A House Is a House for Me, by MaryAnn Hoberman (Penguin Group USA)

The Carrot Seed, by Ruth Krauss (HarperCollins)

Time to Eat, by Steve Jenkins and Robin Page (Houghton Mifflin). Also *Time for a Bath* and *Time to Sleep*

Dinosaurs?! by Lila Prap (NorthSouth Books)

Poetry

A Writing Kind of Day: Poems for Young Poets, by Ralph Fletcher (Boyds Mills Press). Also *Moving Day: Poems About Moving*

I Am the Book, by Lee Bennet Hopkins (Holiday House). Also *Been To Yesterdays: Poems of a Life* (Boyds Mills Press)

Requiem: Poems of the Terezin Ghetto, by Paul Janeczko (Candlewick)

Dear World, by Takayo Noda (Puffin)

BookSpeak! by Laura Purdie Salas (Clarion Books)

This Is Just To Say: Poems of Apology and Forgiveness, by Joyce Sidman (Houghton Mifflin)

BOOKS WITH A DISTINCT SENSE OF PLACE

Picture Books

Very Last First Time, by Jan Andrews (Groundwood)

Where the Forest Meets the Sea, by Jeannie Baker (HarperCollins)

White Water, by Michael S. Bandy and Eric Stein (Candlewick)

Many books by Byrd Baylor, including *The Desert Is Theirs* (Aladdin)

The Great Kapok Tree, by Lynne Cherry (Houghton Mifflin Harcourt)

Miss Rumphius, by Barbara Cooney (Penguin Group USA)

Outside Your Window: A First Book of Nature, by Nicola Davies (Candlewick)

In the Sea, by David Elliot (Candlewick Press)

Snow White in New York, by Fiona French (Oxford)

Stopping by Woods on a Snowy Evening, by Robert Frost, illustrated by Susan Jeffers (Dutton Juvenile)

Box Turtle at Long Pond, by William T. George (HarperCollins)

The Year of the Perfect Christmas Tree, by Gloria Houston (Penguin Group USA)

Wave, by Suzy Lee (Chronicle Books)

My Little Island, by Frane Lessac (HarperCollins)

Where the River Begins, by Thomas Locker (Penguin Group USA)

All the Places to Love, by Patricia MacLachlan (Houghton Mifflin)

Over and Under the Snow, by Kate Messner (Chronicle Books)

The People of Twelve Thousand Winters, by Trinka Hakes Noble (Sleeping Bear Press)

Blackout, by John Rocco (Disney Hyperion Books)

When I Was Young in the Mountains, by Cynthia Rylant (Penguin). Also *Appalachia* (Houghton Mifflin Harcourt) and *Night in the Country* (Atheneum)

All the World, by Liz Garton Scanlon (Beach Lane Books)

Sierra, by Diane Siebert. Also *Mojave, Appalachia, Heartland,* and *Cave* (HarperCollins)

Mufaro's Beautiful Daughters, by John Steptoe (HarperCollins)

Dakota Dugout, by Ann Turner (Aladdin)

Three Days on a River in a Red Canoe, by Vera B. Williams (HarperCollins)

Owl Moon, by Jane Yolen (Penguin)

Novels and Poems

Tuck Everlasting, by Natalie Babbitt (Square Fish)

Watsons Go to Birmingham—1963, by Christopher Paul Curtis (Laurel Leaf)

The One O'Clock Chop, by Ralph Fletcher (Henry Holt)

Anything by Jean Craighead George, especially *Julie of the Wolves* (HarperCollins)

Out of the Dust, by Karen Hesse (Scholastic)

Requiem: Poems of the Terezin Ghetto, by Paul Janeczko (Candlewick)

From the Mixed-up Files of Mrs. Basil E. Frankweiler, by E. L Konigsburg (Atheneum)

The Contender, by Robert Lipsyte (HarperCollins)

Anything by Jack London

Sarah, Plain and Tall, by Patricia MacLachlan (HarperCollins)

Anything by Gary Paulsen

Holes, by Louis Sachar (Yearling)

Glory Be, by Augusta Scattergood (Scholastic Press)

The Hobbit: or There and Back Again, by J. R. R. Tolkien (Houghton Mifflin Harcourt)

Birmingham, 1963, by Carole Boston Weatherford (Wordsong)

TIME

These books contain a vivid or unusual sense of time.

Picture Books

The Two of Them, by Aliki (HarperCollins)

I'm in Charge of Celebrations, by Byrd Baylor (Aladdin)

Forever Friends, by Carin Berger (Greenwillow)

Granpa, by John Burningham (Red Fox)

Everett Anderson's Goodbye, by Lucille Clifton (Holt)

Home Place, by Crescent Dragonwagon (Kensington Publishing)

Time Train, by Paul Fleischman (HarperCollins)

The Secret Box, by Barbara Lehman (Houghton Mifflin)

When I Was Young in the Mountains, by Cynthia Rylant (Penguin Group USA). Also *Night in the Country* (Atheneum Books for Young Readers)

Grandpa Green, by Lane Smith (Roaring Brook Press)

Stevie, by John Steptoe (HarperCollins)

Just a Dream, by Chris Van Allsburg (Houghton Mifflin Harcourt)

The Beatitudes: From Slavery to Civil Rights, by Carole Boston Weatherford (Eerdmans Books for Young Readers)

Flotsam, by David Wiesner (Clarion Books)

Country Dog, City Frog, by Mo Willems (Hyperion)

A Chair for My Mother, by Vera B. Williams (HarperCollins). Flashback

Novels

Autumn Street, by Lois Lowry (Random House Children's Books)

The Wonder of Charlie Anne, by Kimberly Newton Fusco (Knopf)

Julie of the Wolves, by Jean Craighead George (HarperCollins). Flashback

Pictures of Hollis Woods, by Patricia Reilly Giff (Wendy Lamb Books). Also *Eleven*

Turtle in Paradise, by Jennifer L. Holm (Random House Books for Young Readers)

Sarah, Plain and Tall, by Patricia MacLachlan (HarperCollins). Flashback

Wonder, by R. J. Palacio (Knopf Books for Young Readers)

Dogsong, by Gary Paulsen (Simon and Schuster Books for Young Readers). Also *Hatchet*

When You Reach Me, by Rebecca Stead (Wendy Lamb Books)

Moon Over Manifest, by Clare Vanderpool (Yearling)

Countdown, by Debra Wiles (Scholastic)

One Crazy Summer, by Rita Williams-Garcia (Amistad)

A Monster Calls, by Patrick Ness (Candlewick)

TENSION/CONFLICT

Person vs. Person Conflict in Picture Books

Shark vs. Train, by Chris Barton (Little, Brown Books for Young Readers)

Z Is for Moose, by Kelly Bingham (Greenwillow Books)

Old Henry, by Joan W. Blos (HarperCollins)

You Will Be My Friend! by Peter Brown (Little, Brown Books for Young Readers)

Piggybook, by Anthony Browne (Random House Books for Children)

Smoky Night, by Eve Bunting (Sandpiper)

Horsefly and Honeybee, by Randy Cecil (Henry Holt and Company)

Click, Clack, Moo: Cows That Type, by Doreen Cronin (Simon & Schuster)

Llama Llama Mad at Mama, by Anna Dewdney (Viking Juvenile)

Bella and Bean, by Rebecca Kai Dotlich (Atheneum Books for Young Readers)

Lilly's Purple Plastic Purse, by Kevin Henkes (Greenwillow)

All for Me and None for All, by Helen Lester (Houghton Mifflin Books for Children)

Thomas' Snowsuit, by Robert Munsch (Annick Press)

The Big Orange Splot, by Daniel Pinkwater (Scholastic)

I Must Have Bobo! by Eileen Rosenthal (Atheneum Books for Young Readers)

No, David! by David Shannon (Blue Sky Press)

Novels and Short Stories

Chains, by Laurie Halse Anderson (Atheneum). Also *Forge*

Jacob Wonderbar and the Cosmic Space Kapow, by Nathan Bransford (Dial)

Summer of the Swans, by Betsy Byars (Penguin)

No Talking, by Andrew Clements (Atheneum)

Ironman, by Chris Crutcher (Greenwillow)

Elijah of Buxton, by Christopher Paul Curtis (Scholastic Press)

The Lemonade Wars, by Jacqueline Davies (Sandpiper)

Spider Boy, by Ralph Fletcher (Sandpiper). Also *Uncle Daddy* (Holt)

The Loser List, by H. N. Kowitt (Scholastic). Also *The Loser List #2: Revenge of the Loser*

The Call of the Wild, by Jack London (Scholastic)

Number the Stars, by Lois Lowry (Houghton Mifflin Harcourt)

Travel Team, by Mike Lupica (Puffin). Also *Summer Ball*

Kaffir Boy, by Mark Mathabane (Free Press)

The War with Grandpa, by Robert K. Smith (Random House Children's Books)

Naya Nuki: Shoshoni Girl Who Ran, by Kenneth Thomasma (Baker Books)

The Great Wall of Lucy Wu, by Wendy Wan-Long Shang (Scholastic Press)

"The Most Dangerous Game," short story by Richard Connell (Perfection Learning)

PERSON VS. NATURE

Picture Books

Where the Forest Meets the Sea and *Window,* by Jeannie Baker (Greenwillow)

The Great Kapok Tree, by Lynne Cherry (Houghton Mifflin Harcourt)

Otis and the Tornado, by Loren Long (Philomel)

We're Going on a Bear Hunt, by Michael Rosen (Margaret K. McElderry Books)

Brave Irene and *Amos and Boris,* by William Steig (Square Fish)

Just a Dream, by Chris Van Allsburg (Houghton Mifflin Harcourt)

Novels and Short Stories

Julie of the Wolves, by Jean Craighead George (HarperCollins), also *My Side of the Mountain* and *On the Far Side of the Mountain* (Penguin Group USA)

Never Cry Wolf, by Farley Mowat (Little, Brown and Company)

Island of the Blue Dolphins, by Scott O'Dell (Houghton Mifflin Harcourt)

Dogsong, Hatchet, Tracker, and *Woodsong,* by Gary Paulsen (Simon & Schuster Books for Young Readers). Also *Brian's Winter* (Laurel Leaf), *Brian's Hunt* (Laurel Leaf), *Brian's Return* (Laurel Leaf)

"To Build a Fire," short story by Jack London, in *The Collected Jack London,* edited by Steven J. Kasdin (Barnes & Noble)

INNER CONFLICT

Picture Books

Those Shoes, by Maribeth Boelts (Candlewick)

Wemberly Worried, by Kevin Henkes (Greenwillow)

Sister Anne's Hands, by Marybeth Lorbiecki (Puffin)

Annie and the Old One, by Miska Miles (Little, Brown Books for Young Readers)

Emma Dilemma: Big Sister Poems, by Kristine O'Connell George (Clarion Books)

Gila Monsters Meet You at the Airport, by Marjorie Sharmat (Aladdin)

Faithful Elephants, by Yukio Tsuchiya (Houghton Mifflin Harcourt)

Nettie's Trip South, by Ann Turner (Aladdin)

Ira Sleeps Over, by Bernard Waber (Houghton Mifflin Harcourt). Also *Ira Says Goodbye*

Should I Share My Ice Cream? by Mo Willems (Hyperion/DBG)

The Can Man, by Laura E. Williams (Lee & Low Books)

The Other Side, by Jacqueline Woodson (Putnam Juvenile)

Novels and Short Stories

Flying Solo, by Ralph Fletcher (Sandpiper)

One-Eyed Cat, by Paula Fox (Aladdin)

The Candy Corn Contest, by Patricia Reilly Giff (Random House Children's Books). Also *Pictures of Hollis Woods* (Wendy Lamb Books)

Rules, by Cynthia Lord (Scholastic)

Sugar and Ice, by Kate Messner (Walker Children's)

The Fantastic Secret of Owen Jester, by Barbara O'Connor (Farrar, Straus and Giroux)

Bigger than a Bread Box, by Laurel Snyder (Random House Books for Young Readers)

Wringer, by Jerry Spinelli (HarperCollins)

A Solitary Blue, by Cynthia Voigt (Atheneum Books for Young Readers)

The Castle in the Attic, by E. Winthrop (Random House Children's Books)

BOOKS WITH UNFORGETTABLE LANGUAGE

Picture Books

Very Last First Time, by Jan Andrews (Groundwood)

Names for Snow, by Judi K. Beach (Hyperion)

Books by Byrd Baylor, especially *I'm in Charge of Celebrations* (Aladdin)

Fireflies, by Julie Brinckloe (Aladdin Paperbacks)

The Great Kapok Tree, by Lynne Cherry (Houghton Mifflin Harcourt)

Twilight Comes Twice and *Hello, Harvest Moon,* by Ralph Fletcher (Clarion Books)

Moonshot: The Flight of Apollo 11, by Brian Floca (Atheneum: Richard Jackson Books)

And Then It's Spring, by Julie Fogliano (Roaring Book Press)

Birdsongs, by Betsy Franco (Margaret K. McElderry Books)

On the Day You Were Born, by Debra Frasier (Houghton Mifflin Harcourt)

Come On, Rain! by Karen Hesse (Scholastic Press)

The Ghost-Eye Tree, by Bill Martin Jr. (Henry Holt). Also *Listen to the Rain* (Henry Holt)

Grandpa Loved, by Josephine Nobisso (Gingerbread House)

Sit-In: How Four Friends Stood Up by Sitting Down, by Andrea Davis Pinkney (Little, Brown)

Tar Beach, by Faith Ringgold (Random House Children's Books)

In November, by Cynthia Rylant (Harcourt Children's Books). Also *The Relatives Came*

Red Sings from Treetops: A Year in Colors, by Joyce Sidman (Houghton Mifflin)

Sierra, by Diane Siebert (HarperCollins)

Books by William Stieg, especially *Brave Irene* and *Amos and Boris* (Square Fish)

Owl Moon, by Jane Yolen (Penguin Group USA)

Poetry

Jabberwocky, by Lewis Carroll (Kids Can Press)

Joyful Noise: Poems for Two Voices, by Paul Fleischman (HarperCollins)

Dear Hot Dog, by Mordicai Gerstein (Abrams Books for Young Readers)

Honey, I Love, and other poems by Eloise Greenfield (HarperCollins)

"From Mother to Son," poem by Langston Hughes

Requiem: Poems of the Terezin Ghetto, by Paul Janeczko (Candlewick)

Swirl by Swirl: Spirals in Nature, by Joyce Sidman (Houghton Mifflin). Also *Ubiquitous: Celebrating Nature's Survivors* and *Dark Emperor: Other Poems of the Night*

Mirror Mirror: A Book of Reversible Verse, by Marilyn Singer (Dutton Children's Books)

All the Small Poems and Fourteen More, by Valerie Worth (Farrar, Straus and Giroux)

Cousins of Clouds: Elephant Poems, by Tracie Vaughn Zimmer (Clarion Books)

Novels for Young Readers

Wintergirls, by Laurie Halse Anderson (Viking Juvenile)

Tuck Everlasting, by Natalie Babbit (Square Fish)

I Heard the Owl Call My Name, by Margaret Craven (Random House Publishing)

The BFG, by Roald Dahl (Penguin Group USA)

Out of My Mind, by Sharon Draper (Atheneum)

Out of the Dust and *Music of Dolphins,* by Karen Hesse (Scholastic)

"Clothes" and "Oranges" in *Hey World, Here I Am!* by Jean Little (HarperCollins)

Ceremony, by Leslie M. Silko (Penguin Group USA)

Breadcrumbs, by Anne Ursu (Walden Pond Press)

Other Novels

A Death in the Family, by James Agee (Penguin Group USA)

Money, by Martin Amis (Penguin Group USA)

The School of Essential Ingredients and *Joy for Beginners,* by Erica Bauermeister (Putnam)

Woman Hollering Creek, by Sandra Cisneros (Vintage)

An American Childhood, by Annie Dillard (HarperCollins)

Peace Like a River, by Leif Enger (Atlantic Monthly Press)

Love Medicine, by Louise Erdrich (HarperCollins)

Stones from the River, by Ursula Hegi (Simon & Schuster)

Ironweed, by William Kennedy (Penguin Group USA)

The Book of Laughter and Forgetting, by Milan Kundera (HarperCollins)

Native Speaker, by Chang-Rae Lee (Riverhead)

Novels by Toni Morrison, especially *Beloved* (Plume)

Lolita, by Vladimir Nabokov (Vintage)

Bel Canto, by Ann Patchett (Harper Perennial)

Housekeeping, by Marilynne Robinson (Picador)

$\mathcal{I}$NDEX

Abrams, Jessica, 65
Ackerman, Diane, 158–159
Agee, James, 145
Aliki, 15, 51
"All about the Oil Spill" (Loewy), 77
Amis, Martin, 145
Amos and Boris (Steig), 5
Angle of Repose (Stegner), 18
Animal Medical Center (Manhattan), 156
Archambault, John, 149
Art of Fiction, The (Gardner), 26, 119, 124
"Astronomers Find Biggest Black Holes
    Yet" (Overbye), 153
Atticus (Hansen), 145

Babbitt, Natalie, 84
Baker, Jeannie, 98
Baylor, Byrd, 47
Beginnings. *See* Leads
Bel Canto (Patchett), 18
Beloved (Morrison), 102
Bettelheim, Bruno, 87
Bien, Peter, 18
"Boots, The" (Fletcher), 116–117
Boston Bruins, 35
Boston Globe, 35, 172
Boy Scouts, 3–4, 33, 177
Boy Writers: Reclaiming Their Voices
    (Fletcher), 158
Bradbury, Ray, 24
Bragg, Rick, 155–156
Brave Irene (Steig), 110, 111
Breaks, The (Price), 12
Bridge to Terabithia (Paterson), 84
Brooks, Bruce, 157

Bugs (Parker and Wright), 77
"To Build a Fire" (London), 110
Bunting, Eve, 106
Burningham, John, 62, 97–98
A Burnt-Out Case (Greene), 144

Calkins, Lucy, 169
Campanella, Roy, 12
Can We Save The Tiger? (Jenkins), 77
Carver, Raymond, 20, 145
A Chair for My Mother (Williams), 133
Chandler, Raymond, 22
Character, 55–66; in the beginning, 86;
    conflict reveals, 110–111; details of,
    59–60, 63–64, 123; developing, 4;
    "dump truck" writing, 77; flash-draft,
    64–66; flesh out, 57–59; main, 98;
    narrator development of, 68; nonfiction
    and, 64–66; persona of, 57–59; reader
    identification with, 56; reconcile
    internal conflict with, 111; setting and,
    119, 123; tension and, 105–106; voice
    and, 68, 69
Charlotte's Web (White), 38, 84, 98, 166
Charybdis (sea monster), 2
Chekhov, Anton, 51, 145
Chesterton, G.K, 80
"Christmas That Wasn't, The" (Fletcher), 83
Cinderella, 51
Cisneros, Sandra, 181
Clam digging, 120–121
Clockers (Price), 12
Cohen, Robert, 16, 122
Collins, Anie, 41
Color of Money, The (Price), 12

Conflict: internal, 111–112; person vs nature, 106, 110–111; person vs person, 105–106; tension and, 105. *See also* Tension

Consistency, in writing, 129

Cosmopolitan magazine, 13, 157

Coyne, Pamela, 11

Curtis, JoAnn, 20, 38, 63, 71, 128, 146, 171, 172–175. *See also* Portalupi, JoAnn

Dahl, Roald, 81

Damon, Mrs., 11

"Dead Wrong" (Fletcher), 172–175

"Death and Rebirth in the Change of a Name" (Fletcher), 170–172

dePaola, Tomie, 166

Details, 45–54; character, 59–60, 63–64, 123; concrete, 47–48; envoking large issues, 49–50; physical, 46; recurring, 51–54

Dialogue: eavesdrop, 61–62; spoken, 62, 84; student fiction, 26

Digital Writing, 179–181

Digital Writing Workshop, The (Hicks), 179

Dillard, Annie, 69, 70, 145

Discovery, writing as, 21–23

Donleavy, J. P., 78

Dr. Seuss, 4

"Dump-truck" writing, 77

Duncan, Robert, 104

East of Eden (Steinbeck), 145

Elbow, Peter, 67

Element: literary, 3; of surprise, 40, 88; of time, 127–133, 138–141; of writing, 5, 56

Eliot, T. S., 96

Emotion, in writing, 18, 28, 32, 101, 123

Ending, 93–103; ambiguous, 97–98; as beginning, 85–86; circular, 95–96; expository writing, 94; ironic, 101–103; poignant, 98–101; surprise, 94–95

Esposito, Phil, 35

Even Cowgirls Get the Blues (Robbins), 25

Expository writing, 94

Faithful Elephants (Tsuchiya), 106

Farrell, James T., 10

A Father Like That (Zolotow), 101

"Feature writing," 156

Fig Pudding (Fletcher), 83

"First Shave is the Closet, The" (Fletcher), 90–92

Fisher, David, 13

Fishman, Steve, 11

Fitzgerald, F. Scott, 22, 127

"Five-Dollar Job, The," 181–182

Flashback, 133

Flash-draft, 64–66

Fletcher, Freddy, 63

Flying Solo (Fletcher), 111–112, 133

Focus, in writing, 138–139

"Food chain," 45

Ford, Richard, 145

Foreshadowing, 88

Four Quartets (Elliot), 96

Fox (Wild), 111

Frasier, Debra, 40

"Friday Night at the Spider Fights" (Fletcher), 159

Fry, Nan, 14

Fuentes, Carlos, 31

Fuller, Buckminster, 32

Gardinier, Suzanne, 72

Gardner, John, 26, 124

George, Jean Craighead, 123

Ghost-Eye Tree, The (Martin), 96, 113, 149

Gibson, William, 40

"Gift of the Magi, The" (Henry), 95

Gila Monsters Meet You at the Airport (Sharmat), 86, 114

Ginott, Haim, 9

Ginsberg, Allen, 5

"Go Waste, Young Man" (Michener), 178
Godwin, Gail, 153
Going After Cacciato (O'Brien), 12
Goodnight Mr. Tom (Magorian), 84
Graduate, The (Willingham), 9
Granpa (Burningham), 62, 97
Graves, Don, 3
Great Gatsby, The (Fitzgerald), 127
Green, Pumpsie, 46
Greene, Graham, 144
Greenfield, Eloise, 33
Gregory, Bill, 57
Grosman, Tanya, 32, 156, 157

*Half The Sky: Turning Oppression Into
    Opportunity For Women Worldwide*
    (Kristof and YuDunn), 178
Hamsun, Knut, 18
Handwriting, 11
Hansen, Ron, 145
Harrods of London, 156, 157
Hatchet (Paulsen), 111, 133
Hawkins, Vanessa, 149
Hazen, Barbara Shook, 105–106
Healy, Mary K., 77
Hemingway, Ernest, 129
Henry, O., 95
Heroes (McGinniss), 104
Hicks, Troy, 179
Honesty, in writing, 14, 16, 20, 25–26, 82,
    112
Honey, I Love (Greenfield), 33
"Hot spots," in writing and movies, 140,
    141
Howell, Karen, 6
Hughes, Langston, 96, 149
Hunger (Hamsun), 18
Hyman, Trina Schart, 106

I Am Wings: Poems About Love (Fletcher),
    166–168

I Stink! (McMullan), 77
Ignorance, in writing, 157
Illustrations, 26, 51, 106
I'm in Charge of Celebrations (Baylor), 47
Imagery, in writing, 32, 47
Insight: factual, 158–161; intelligent, 154;
    interpretive, 161–164
Inspirations from writers, 145
Inspired Sleep (Cohen), 16, 122
Irony, in writing, 101–102
Irving, John, 147
It's Good to be Alive (Campanella), 12

Jackson, Shirley, 89
Jaws (movie), 110
Jenkins, Martin, 77
Jobs, Steve, 178
Jody, Marilyn, 22
Johns, Jasper, 32
Jordan, Michael, 178
Joyce, James, 18, 55
Julie of the Wolves (George), 123, 133
Jurassic Park (movie), 110

Kafka, Franz, 71, 181
Kazantzakis, Nikos, 18
Keeping Quilt, The (Polacco), 139
Kennedy, Jack, 42
Kerouac, Jack, 13
Kesey, Ken, 12, 18
King, Stephen, 18
Kristof, Nicholas, 178
Kundera, Milan, 181

Langerstrom, Janette, 173
Language: book, 18; love of words, 31–42;
    specific, 47–48; students use, 25;
    unforgettable, 144–153. *See also* Words
Lanning, George, 153
Lao Tzu, 82
"Last Kiss, The" (Fletcher), 28–30

Lawrence, D. H., 12

Leads, 81–92; ambiguous, 89–92; auditory clue, 83–84; beginning at the ending, 85–86, 96; dramatic, 82–83; first steps, 82; flashback, 132–133; foreshadowing, 88; leisurely, 84–85; middle of a scene, 83–84; misleading, 88–89; narrator introduction as, 86–88; reflective tone, 85; scene, 122; strategies, 87–88; tension, 114–115

Leaves of Grass (Whitman), 86

L'Engle, Madeleine, 95

Lenz, Lisa, 149, 151

Lie Down in Darkness (Styron), 104

Linear time, 131

"Line of experience" (Fletcher), 138–139

Linguistic stranglehold, 36

Little Big Man (Willingham), 9

Loewy, Lauren, 77

London, Jack, 110

"Long Trip" (Hughes), 149

Lorax, The (Seuss), 4

Lord of the Flies, 51

"Lottery, The" (Jackson), 89

Louis the Fish (Yorinks), 86

Lum, Darrell H.Y., 33

Macauley, Robie, 153

MacLachlan, Patricia, 84

Magorian, Michelle, 84

Mann, Thomas, 13, 145

Mantilla, Félix, 46

Márquez, Gabriel García, 12

Martin, Bill Jr., 80, 96, 113, 149

Martinez, Christine, 15

Matilda (Dahl), 81

Maxwell, William, 145

McCullers, Carson, 122

McFlintock, Cory, 70

McGinniss, Joe, 104

McMullan, Kate, 77

McMurphy, Randall, 56

Member of the Wedding, The (McCullers), 122

"Mentor texts," 19

Mentors, 9–20; novels as, 12

Merton, Andrew, 78

Metaphors: image and, 6, 161; mixed, 26, 115; tension in, 115

Michener, James, 165, 178

Miss Alaineus: A Vocabulary Disaster (Frasier), 40

Miss Maggie (Rylant), 60

Moby Dick, 86

"Moiliili Bag Man, The" (Lum), 33

Monbouquette, Bill, 46

Money (Amis), 145

Morrison, Toni, 102

Mud puppy, 35–36

Murray, Donald, 2, 19, 46, 47, 129, 158, 170, 172, 181

Museum of Natural History, 156

My Turn at Bat (Williams), 12

Nabokov, Vladimir, 145

Nader, Ralph, 178

A Natural History of the Senses (Ackerman), 158–159

Nettie's Trip South (Turner), 106

Neuromancer (Gibson), 40

New Advocate, The (Fletcher), 169

New York Times magazine, 153

New Yorker, The magazine, 155

Niffenegger, Audrey, 18

1984 (Orwell), 102

Nonfiction writing, 1–2, 154; exploratory writing in, 78–80; facts, 158–161; passion, 76; techniques for, 77–78; Type A and Type B, 78–80; voice in, 76–78

Norris, Frank, 12

Novels: inspired to write by, 18; as mentors, 12

Nye, Naomi Shihab, 168–169

Obama, Barack, 84
O'Brien, Tim, 12
Odysseus, 2
Odyssey, The (Homer), 95
Oerter, Al, 156, 157
O'Hara, Scarlett, 56
Old Gringo, The (Fuentes), 31
"Olympics: Skeleton" (Bragg), 155–156
Omission, in writing, 133–138
One Flew Over the Cuckoo's Nest (Kesey), 12
One Hundred Years of Solitude (Márquez), 12
One O'Clock Chop, The (Fletcher), 121, 166
"One Piece of My Father" (Panciera), 55
One Writer's Beginnings (Welty), 32
Orr, Bobby, 35
Orwell, George, 102
Outlines, 21, 23, 78
Overbye Dennis, 153
Owen, David, 155
Owl Moon (Yolen), 3, 47
Oz, Amos, 127

Panciera, Carla, 55
Panzarella, Joseph. Dr., 49
Paperboy (Pilkey), 138
Park, Andrew, 149
Parker, Nancy Winslow, 77
Passion, in writing, 18, 76
Patchett, Ann, 18
Paterson, Katherine, 84
Paulsen, Gary, 33, 111
Pedone, Gina, 74–75
Penmanship, 11
People magazine, 49
Phillips, Jayne Anne, 177
Picture books: concrete examples in, 3, 87; conflict through, 105–106, 110, 111, 114; endings of, 97; language through, 19, 62; referenced, 5, 51, 60
Piggy, 51

Pikey, Dav, 138
Pilgrim at Tinker Creek (Dillard), 69
Place, 118–127; discovery of, 22; snapshots, 132. *See also* Setting
Plumer, Mr., 35
Poe, Edgar Allen, 87
"Poem" (Hughes), 96
Polacco, Patricia, 139
Portalupi, JoAnn, 64, 129, 147, 174. *See also* Curtis, JoAnn
Price, Richard, 12, 14, 49, 140

Rauschenburg, Robert, 32
Reader's Digest, 158
Redbook magazine, 24–25
Rejection notices, 2, 25
Relatives Came, The (Rylant), 96, 114, 144
Resistance, 114
Revision, in writing, 165–166, 168–169
Rexroth, Kenneth, 13
Rilke, Rainer Maria, 178
Risk-taking: students and, 25, 27; teachers and, 130–131; as a writer, 4, 17, 24
"River Heart" (Fletcher), 53–54
Rivers, Larry, 32
Robbins, Tom, 25
Rosenblatt, Louise, 97
Rylant, Cynthia, 32, 60, 70–71, 96, 114, 132, 144, 145

Sarah, Plain and Tall (MacLachlan), 84, 133
Scene: dramatic, 140; flash-draft, 64; leads, 83; place, 122; symmetry, 69; time and, 140–141
Scieszka, Jon, 87
Scylla (sea monster), 2
Setting, 118–126; backdrop and integral, 122–124; character and, 119; classroom, 14; developed through five senses, 120–121; elements of writing, 5, 56; student writing, 26, 119. *See also* Place

Seuss, Dr., 4
Shacochis, Bob, 161
Shannon, Patrick, 17
Sharmat, Marjorie, 86, 114
Sheriff, Valerie, 41
Simic, Charles, 115
Singer, Isaac B., 119
Smith, Red, 21
Smith, Robert Kimmel, 105
Smith Winston, 102
Smoky Nights (Bunting), 106
Snapshots, 132
Snyder, Gary, 5
Solander, in writing, 153, 154
Solnit, Rebecca, 118
Sometimes a Great Notion (Kesey), 18
Spampinato, Erin, 151
Spider Boy (Fletcher), 159
Spirit Makes a Man (Panzarella), 49
Stafford, William, 168
Stegner, Wallace, 18
Steig, William, 5, 110
Steinbeck, John, 145
Steptoe, John, 98
Stevie (Steptoe), 98
Stock, Robert, 13
Student writing: age affects, 146–147;
    element of time in, 130–131; nonfiction
    and, 157–158; topics for, 157
Styron, William, 104
Subject: exploratory writing, 78–79;
    importance of, 4, 6, 157; lead, 82, 88;
    new place, 22; nonfiction, 154–155;
    students and, 27–28; voice and, 72, 74

Tallmountain, Mary, 45
Tattoos, 157
Teaching: character and, 57, 58;
    environment and, 28; importance of
    words, 36–38; language and, 149; praise
    and, 25; revision, 169–170; rewriting

voice, 72, 78, 80; risk, 130–131, 170;
    slices of time, 138, 141; using powerful
    images, 150–151; voice, 68, 78–79
Technique in Fiction (Macauley and
    Lanning), 153
"Tell-Tale Heart, The" (Poe), 87
Tension, 104–116. *See also* Conflict
Thompson, Mr., 35
Thoreau, 69–70
Tight Times (Hazen), 105–106
Time: control of, 129–130; discovery of,
    130; flashback, 132–133; focus, 138–
    139; linear, 131–132; omission, 133,
    138; real vs story, 130–131; slowing of,
    139–141; snapshots of, 132; to write,
    127, 128
Time-Traveler's Wife, The (Niffenegger), 18
Titanic (movie), 110
"Toll Booth Woman" (Fletcher), 102–103
Tomarelli, Nicki, 93–94
Topic: risky and safe, 28; significance in,
    157; trapdoor, 24
Transactional theory of literature, 97–98
True Story of the Three Little Pigs, The
    (Scieszka), 87
Tsuchiya, Yukio, 106
Tuck Everlasting (Babbitt), 84
Turner, Ann, 106
Twain, Mark, 33, 177–178
Twilight Comes Twice (Fletcher), 19
Two of Them, The (Aliki), 15, 51

"Unifying simplicities" (Murray), 2
Universal Limited Arts Editions Studio, 32
Unsafe At Any Speed (Nader), 178

Vocabulary, 36–38
Voice, 67–80; audience, 72; authentic, 74;
    of authority, 75; dealing with facts,
    159–160; defined, 68; developing,
    68; emotion, 28; facts and, 160–161;

human, 84, 93; humor and, 86; inner, 69–72; intimacy, 74; learning process and, 80; "mentor texts," 19; nonfiction, 76–78, 161; personality on paper, 78; resistance, 114; teaching, 28; tension and, 114–115; "Type A" and "Type B," 78–79; writing and, 72, 74–76

Voigt, Artie, 16, 18

Walking Trees (Fletcher), 35
"Walt Disney," 66
War With Grandpa (Robert Smith), 105
Water Planet (Fletcher), 34
"Watermelons" (Simic), 115
Watson, Jerry, 122
"Waves" (Fletcher), 34
Weiss, Janet, 62
Wells, Linda, Dr., 47
Welty, Eudora, 32, 93, 119–120
When I Was Young in the Mountains (Rylant), 132
Where the Forest Meets the Sea (Baker), 98
Where the Wild Things Are (book), 95
White, E. B., 38, 84, 98, 166
Whitman, Walt, 86
Wild, Margaret, 111
Williams, Ted, 12, 42
Willie Mays Story, The, 12
Willingham, Calder, 9–10
Wire, The (Price), 12
Wizard of Oz, The, 41, 114
Wolf, Alexander T., 87
"Won't You Come Home Bill Bailey?" (Fletcher), 166–167, 170
Woolf, Virginia, 13, 145
Wordplay, 40–41
Words, 31–42; core of writing, 180; define writers, 20; as details, 48; emotion from, 12, 31–32; favorite, 34–35; importance of, 36–37; as labels, 6; meaning of, 34; precision with, 6; primal tools, 36; spoken, 60–63; vocabulary of, 36–38, 149; wordplay, 40–42; writer's notebook

of, 34–35; writer's tools, 32; written, 68. *See also* Language; Writing
Wordsworth, William, 145
World According to Garp (Irving), 147
World Book Encyclopedia, 35
Wright, Joan Richards, 77
A Wrinkle in Time (L'Engle), 95
"Writerly writers," 145
Writers: consistency, 129; inspiration from, 145; mentoring young, 9–20
Writer's notebook, 34, 69, 158, 181
Writing: areas of expertise, 1–2; consistency, 129; details in, 49–53, 59–60; digital, 179–181; as discovery, 21–23; "dump-truck," 77; elements, 5–6; emotion and, 18, 28, 32, 101, 123; exercises, 3, 4, 78, 124, 138; exploration for, 177–178; expository, 94; focus in, 138–139; food chain, 45; foreshadowing, 88; freelance, 156–158; honesty and, 14, 16, 20, 25–26, 82, 112; ignorance in, 157; imagery in, 32, 47; insight, 161; ironic, 101–102; language and, 32–33; leads, 82–92; logic, 23; movement in, 63–64; outlines, 21, 23; passion, 18, 76; penmanship as, 11; power of, 12; risk and, 17, 25, 27, 130–131; setting, 119; specific, 47–48; time, 138; voice in, 69–72
On Writing (King), 18
Writing exercises, 3, 4, 78, 124, 138
Writing to Learn (Zinsser), 78
Writing with Power (Elbow), 67

Yaddo, 128
Yolen, Jane, 3, 32, 37, 47, 70–71, 95
Yorinks, Arthur, 86
Young, Whitney, Jr., 40
YuDunn, Sheryl, 178

Zibulsky, Pat, 89
Zinsser, William, 23, 78, 89
Zolotow, Charlotte, 101